Great
Little
Gardens

Anthony Noel

Special Photography by Andrew Lawson

FRANCES LINCOLN

To Annabel and Richard with love

Frances Lincoln Limited
4 Torriano Mews
Torriano Avenue
London NW5 2RZ

Great Little Gardens
Copyright © Frances Lincoln Limited 1999
Text copyright © Anthony Noel 1999
Photographs copyright © Andrew Lawson 1999 except those listed on page 136
First Frances Lincoln edition: 1999
All rights reserved.

British Library Cataloguing in Publication Data
A catalogue record for this book is available from the British Library.
ISBN 0 7112 1436 0
1 3 5 7 5 9 8 4 2

Printed and bound by KHL Printing Co Pte ltd, Singapore

Contents

Foreword by Brenda Blethyn

Tony Noel has been my friend for nearly thirty years, ever since we met at the Guildford School of Acting. We were both struggling hopefuls then, with nothing more than a pocket full of dreams between us. Of our year, he has been one of the most successful.

At drama school he was always a bit of a lost soul, but he had an inner calm the rest of us did not possess. While he had little confidence in himself, I had total confidence in him; I always knew he was a man with a vision. If ever I was doubting myself, he was the person I would seek. It was obvious to me, even then, that his creative talent and inner calm would take him a long way.

But what a surprising route! Tony's stages are not the theatres of Shaftesbury Avenue and Broadway, but the smallest balcony, rooftop or backyard. He brings all the qualities I most enjoy in the theatre to everything from the grandest hotel to a garden made for two: glamour, mystery, drama, romance and humour. His gardens are made with immaculate taste and simplicity; they are beautifully detailed, but never precious. As in a good play, even the smallest parts are well cast, and they are always full of surprises and twists.

I remember that when I saw his first garden, I knew my instincts about him had been proved right. I was amazed to find such calm in the heart of town. It was as modern as tomorrow but had this sense of history. I loved the attention to detail and the patient, calm way he had guided the whole production. The crumbling grandeur of his gardens is never over the top, for they always have the qualities of simplicity and tranquillity.

Tony is an entertainer through and through and he makes gardens fun; they feel secure and yet not overstructured. They are a joy to share with friends or just to sit in alone. He seems to be able to create a contemporary drama or a historical one, but it is always set with a light-hearted dash of romance.

I love his drawings too – beautiful and quirky, like his gardens. This book modestly shows you how to follow in his footsteps with apparent ease – it is hardly surprising that he is considered one of Britain's most creative and innovative garden designers.

Even with his success, he remains one of the gentlest, kindest, most unassuming people I know. I hope you enjoy this book as much as I do. Long may our friendship continue.

How I Became a Gardener

Once the packing-cases are emptied, how many of us know that feeling of despair at the prospect of making a garden? The fences are all broken-down, there is a rotten tree-stump between you and the next-door neighbour and any paths that exist are made of cracked concrete that puddles in just the wrong place. To make matters worse, your main 'view' is a jumble of pipes, net curtains and peeling paint. And the sun just seems to miss your plot. What do you do? Admit defeat and move to somewhere with no garden? Or look upon the whole thing as a challenge and try to work it out? Other people have done it – why should they be any more capable than you or me? It is simply a matter of confidence and determination. If you need further convincing, take a look at the pictures in this book, but, before I tell you how the transformations came about, I would like to describe where I began.

My love affair with gardens started when I was four years old at my grandparents' Regency house on the Devonshire coast. They bought the Dunmore just after the Second World War and turned it into one of the first country-house hotels. Even at that age, I realized that the low stuccoed building, with its semicircular colonnaded porch, arched windows and verandas dripping with evergreen magnolia and wisteria, was something special.

We used to approach the house along steep country lanes, barely wide enough for two cars to pass each other. The first thing you saw, near the entrance to the drive, was an old-fashioned walled

My grandparents' house, the Dunmore, as I remember it. This is where my passion for gardening began.

garden complete with greenhouses, espaliers, cold-frames and potting-sheds. Here, my uncle was starting a market-garden business with his young actress wife. Sometimes, as a special treat, I was allowed in the greenhouses. There were peaches, nectarines and grapes; geraniums for the house and a Victorian dipping-well; but the things I remember most were the warm, damp smell of the earth under whitewashed glass and, outside, an ancient mulberry tree with sheets laid on the ground to catch the ripe fruit at the end of each summer.

Behind the house was a tunnel leading to a sandy cove we called The Ness – once, legend had it, used by smugglers. Near the tunnel's entrance my grandmother had made a private cottage garden, overflowing with old-fashioned flowers and complete with a secret, magic pond.

One afternoon, as children do, I must have wandered off from the others and found myself at the front of the house, away from the sea. Looking back I saw the gracious architecture of the Dunmore, perfect in its setting of hanging beechwoods and mossy lawns. Eventually, I came upon a lavender hedge that was as tall as I was. It felt like the jungle as I battled my way through the hundreds of scented flowers that almost covered the narrow steps leading down to a small, sunken garden.

At the far end was a rustic thatched gazebo, and in the centre, a rectangular pool set into crazy-paving, surrounded by rose beds. And there, on a small island that had once been a fountain, stood my elder brother Richard, daring me to jump. Sadly, I do not suppose I would give the little garden a second glance today but, away from parental eyes and with a toy sailing-boat to play with, we thought this was a marvellous place.

Five years later, when I was nine, my mother took me to Sissinghurst, in Kent, where I met Vita Sackville-West. She was weeding in the Tower Garden and, although I cannot remember the conversation, I thought she was very nice, quietly spoken and patient. I loved the romantic ruined castle and the way the garden had been conceived as a series of rooms linked by vistas. The generosity of the planting reminded me of Devon, but of course the quality at Sissinghurst was far, far more sophisticated. There were black flowers, striped flowers and treasures growing in reclaimed stone sinks. Impossibly deep borders of clashing violets, purples and shocking-pinks – as modern as anything in Manhattan, but rich as old Venetian brocade.

The Cottage Garden, the Moat Walk, the Lime Walk – everything lavish, yet casual and set off by immaculately clipped dark green yew hedges. Then through the simple Kentish orchard and just when you thought any more beauty would be too much to bear – there it was: the White Garden. White-hot with glamour, it made this nine-year-old foolish with its beauty. It beckons still. Sissinghurst was then, and still is for me, one of the wonders of the world.

But it was the compartments at another great garden, Hidcote in Gloucestershire, that first taught me not to accept the limitations of a small space. I was a teenager when I saw it first. I immediately liked the playful formality of large squares of box flanking the front door and the pure enchantment of the modest lion's mask fountain on

Lupins, lilies and roses rise above box hedges in this corner of the White Garden at Sissinghurst, which first mesmerized me when I was nine years old.

the barn wall opposite; both ideas I that have used since in smaller places. Although much of it is grand, Hidcote has a sort of home-made quality that allows many of the details to be copied elsewhere: mossy stone sinks set in a border to give a change in level; old watering-cans decorating a flight of steps with clipped *Cotoneaster horizontalis* covering the risers; agaves and cordylines set out for the summer in the palm garden.

While many of these small-scale ideas are ideal for smaller gardens, even the grander things inspired me: the trellis walls (a marvellous idea where space and money are at a premium); large urns and old French garden furniture in smoky-blue. Even hornbeams on stilts and pavilions – scaled down – are not impossible ideas for smaller spaces. But for me, the most memorable sight on that first visit was a small square of exquisitely frail pink-and-white cyclamen in the dry shade of an old cedar of Lebanon where nothing much else would grow. You could adapt this to the shadiest, smallest garden.

The story of my own first garden, in Fulham, begins in 1986 on an empty stage. When I was an actor work was always hard to come by, but rehearsals had just started on a pantomime in the West Country and I was assistant stage-manager. Unfortunately my coat developed a hole in the

10

ABOVE *One of the outside rooms, in this case the White Garden at Hidcote.*
RIGHT *My first great little garden in early summer.*

pocket through which I lost my season-ticket to London and I was stuck in Bath. Unable to get home, I borrowed the money from the company manager to rent what could loosely be called a flat. It was so cold that, even with all the rings and the oven of the wretched cooker turned on full, your breath looked like smoke as it hit the air. Sleeping fully-clothed in the middle of the night, it struck me that there might be more to life than the theatre; I went back to London. There, I needed a job.

An old friend, Laura, came to the rescue. 'Why don't you help me with my new garden and, with the money you earn, what about improving this place?' she said, glancing at the dreary surroundings of my garden. 'You could repair the walls, break up the concrete and take down that awful washing-line!'

They were exciting times. I started, as Laura suggested, by breaking up the concrete. The plot was 'L'-shaped and, as it was only 12m/39ft long by 5m/17ft wide, I knew that it would not be hard to pave the top of the 'L' – the area by the back door – in old bricks. I took them from skips and laid them directly on earth, like the ones I had seen at Sissinghurst and Hidcote. If there was the odd wobble, who cared? It would only add to the effect!

I was left with the main area to deal with. After several false starts, I worked out that it was possible to form a vista from the back window, through the small brick yard and finishing at a disused gate that had once led to a long-demolished mews.

There was just enough room to form a secondary, horizontal axis by placing a chair

RIGHT *Inspired by the White Garden at Sissinghurst and with a little help from the snow...*

half-way down the left-hand wall – opposite a water-feature similar to the one I had seen in the entrance courtyard at Hidcote. Admittedly Hidcote's was grander (the water falls first into a decorative basin then overflows into an ancient horse-trough, whereas mine splashed straight on to cobbles in an old kitchen sink!). But in both cases a wall-mounted lion's mask is the source for water to fall into a container: the idea is the same. I framed my London fountain with squares of clipped box, similar to the ones I had seen flanking the front door at Hidcote. Why not?

I was determined to have a lawn. Expert thinking has always been that an area of turf in a tiny space is impractical. Rules are meant to be broken, however, and I knew that if I made a mowing-strip of old York stone around the square of grass, it would not only reinforce the vista but also form a path by which to return to the house. (It is true that I removed it in the end, but only because I opened the garden for charity quite often and did not like to ask visitors to keep to the paths.) A 1.8m/6ft urn copied from one at Hidcote (in turn probably inspired by the urns at Versailles), set on a raised bed in the far corner, completed the garden's bones. The architecture was vital if the garden was not to be overwhelmed by the surrounding cityscape.

Hungry for knowledge, expertise and new ideas, I read everything I could on gardening, architecture and the decorative arts and visited as many houses and gardens as possible. After ten years my garden had reached its peak, but I was out-growing the little ground-floor flat, the place that had turned my world upside down. It was time to move on.

Playing with
Space
&
Scale

A garden does not have to be large for you to make the most of perspective, space and scale: it is possible to create bold vistas and outlines even in a tiny area. Use the space beyond as a backdrop or screen an unsightly view with trellis, which itself can provide decoration. Play with illusion using *trompe l'oeil*, or take a visitor's breath away – and increase the apparent size of your space – with overscaled shapes. These tricks, used with imagination and confidence, can bring visual impact and variation to a small garden.

THE SKY IS YOUR CEILING

Scale hinges on one golden rule: the sky is your ceiling. With the blue infinity of the sky dictating the terms, simple, bold outlines, vistas and shapes are vital. However beautiful your plants and flowers, they need a strong backdrop to display them at their best. Clean, simple lines always look

sophisticated. Do not worry that the effect will be hard; plants will do all the necessary softening and they look doubly effective when contained within an elegant, formal framework.

I have always admired the American interior decorator and garden designer Nancy Lancaster (1898-1992). This garden I designed with its owner, Mrs Adams, owes much to her laburnum walk (above) at Haseley Court, Oxfordshire. The walk is part of a country walled garden, but the formal structure would work equally well in town. A double row of laburnums flanks a long, straight path terminated by a bench. Adding interest on either side of a vista does not detract from its length, as you might imagine, but can actually make it seem longer. It is important that a path or vista leads somewhere.

In my garden, a strong main vista leads to a seating area dominated by an ornamental urn while a silver-leaved willow, always kept lightly pruned, offers privacy and shade along the path. Being much smaller than the laburnum walk however, it needed even more interest within the space. Varying the paving and flanking the path with details like metal rose pyramids, box topiary and a collection of old pots, allowed the garden to retain its charm but maintains the viewer's interest. The simple, bold structure works with the objects within the garden to make a clean but pretty vista.

FAR LEFT AND
LEFT *The bold line
of a 'long' walk can
be a striking feature
of even a small space.
At Haseley Court
(far left), a double
row of laburnums is
underplanted in
lilac, yellow and
white, and in this
garden I designed
(left) the clean sweep
of the path is
softened by the
variety of pots,
paving, pyramids and
planting. In each, the
visual interest along
the way makes the
walk seem longer
than it really is.*

THE SPACE BEYOND

BELOW *Framing
the view with the
evergreen trees and
the strong, but
elegant, balustrade
makes this balcony
even better.
Everything just falls
into place.*

When you are deciding what sort of garden you would like to create, it is worth giving some thought to the view beyond. Is there a distant church spire, interesting roof- and chimney-scape or even a skyscraper you could echo or frame with bold planting in your garden? If there is, you might be able to work with it; alternatively, and unfortunately, there could be something hideous you need to block out with subtle screening foliage.

Most people's first thought is one of seclusion – and gardens should be secluded – but a secluded garden does not necessarily have to exclude everything outside it. By softening or blurring your garden's boundaries you can take in the surrounding space and so enlarge your own; this effect can even make your garden seem like a compartment in a bigger one. Is there room to plant a small tree in your garden to echo another in a garden beyond? Perhaps your neighbour has planted a climber on

the other side of the fence, for example? Placing a complementary shrub at its foot on your side would give the illusion that your garden continues beyond its actual boundary. Think about matching or contrasting colours. If your neighbour had planted a lilac wisteria, could you plant a soft-yellow *Rosa* 'Mermaid' nearby? They would be a particularly charming combination. The more decorated with plants and shrubs your fences or walls, the softer – and therefore less apparent – they are.

If you are lucky enough to have a view, however spectacular, it will need some sort of screen (ideally walls and fences or dramatic architectural plants) on either side to frame it. If the view is not particularly attractive, the best thing to do might be to break the prospect up by creating a light woodland effect in the foreground. This allows tantalizing glimpses through the leaves and foliage but keeps the main focus within the garden. If you live in a windswept area, and especially if your garden is on a roof, any planted screen will have a practical as well as a decorative purpose: a good group of solid trees or shrubs close together will act as a filter. They will also give a feeling of enclosure.

Whatever the surroundings, within the garden itself the great thing is to use planting and architecture to create a strong uncluttered foreground. This will prevent an enclosed garden from feeling overwhelmed by surrounding buildings, and will enhance a space with a spectacular view.

If your garden is in a city, the chances are that your backdrop will be largely made up of angular roofs and straight lines. Rounded shapes, whether natural or formed by topiary, will make an attractive contrast with the buildings beyond; you could, perhaps, add the odd spiky plant to echo the diagonal lines of the roofs.

ABOVE *Here the hard line of the distant roofs is disguised by the woodland effect in the foreground. The plants give interest to a view that would be bare without them, as well as protecting visitors from the wind and creating a feeling of seclusion.*

TRICKS WITH TRELLIS

The French do clever things with trellis. They understand how to use it decoratively, as exterior wallpaper, without the addition of plants. Sometimes in a Parisian street you come across a blank wall six or eight storeys high and the whole thing has been turned into an architectural fantasy of treillage: columns, false perspective windows and cornices so intricate and pretty that they take your breath away. At Versailles, in the garden of the Petit Trianon, there is a pavilion exquisitely decorated up to the roof, then topped with urns. In the main gardens of the palace, too, trellis is used to create the different outside rooms that make Versailles the ultimate glamorous garden. There are lessons for us here: we can re-create some of their elegance in even the smallest space.

Trellis is good for small gardens because it has such a light touch that it hardly ever becomes oppressive. I have used it to top a boundary wall to a height of 2.75m/9ft (to give privacy) in a garden that was only 5.5m/18ft wide. At that height, trellis needs to be covered in plants, but up to about 2.1m/7ft you could just as easily back it with close-boarded fencing and leave it bare – the effect would not be too strong, even without climbers.

Even the tiniest rooms will appear larger with a lightly patterned wallpaper – perhaps suggesting a rose arbour or trellis – than with plain white walls. This is because the light, decorative lines come forward to catch the eye, while the plain background recedes. Real trellis outside has the same effect.

Trellis's regular squares and pretty shadows make a light setting for the curves of urns, statuary and plants. Also, the regular module seems to increase the feeling of space, acting like a tiled floor. By increasing the apparent area of the walls, you are automatically increasing the size of the garden.

Strangely enough, diamond-patterned or diagonally squared trellis does not seem to work in gardens. It feels as if it

BELOW AND RIGHT *In this city roof garden, the soft blue-grey trellis works well with the sky and disguises the rather ugly brick. The unbroken horizontal lines of the trellis increase the sense of space and provide a flattering background to the plants.*

might take off at any moment. The exception that proves the rule is when diamond shapes are part of the decoration in an architectural fantasy. Plain squares are quieter and harmonize better with the plants and house. The beauty of the material, after all, is that it provides a quiet, elegant background with the feeling of space beyond.

Generally speaking, trellis looks better stained rather than painted; the natural wood seems to demand it. You will not do better than to copy the French colours: darkest green against a background of creamy white is a classic combination. The trellis on the little pavilion at the Petit Trianon is a sort of putty colour, and again the background is creamy white. The general colour at Versailles, apart from dark green, is that wonderful washed-out blue-green that looks so good in a garden setting, enhancing the plants like nothing else. It is also fantastic in a lighter version on a roof garden where the colour's whimsical quality harmonizes with the sky. In this situation, dark green would be too heavy and feel as if one were trying too hard. Slightly warmer, but still light and sophisticated beside creamy white, putty also looks terrific with very pale pink.

Finally, I should add that a 13cm/5in centre with battens that are 3cm/1¼in wide makes a nice proportion for trellis. Trellis with a larger central space takes on too rustic an appearance, and anything smaller can look fussy.

ILLUSIONS OF SPACE

I have always loved the idea of creating a little fantasy to add an extra dimension to a small space. To succeed, it has to be well done, but in a light-hearted, theatrical manner. The illusion should make you smile.

Mirrors can be charming; a panel of them suggesting a classical widow at the end of a vista can look great, especially if it is slightly overgrown with plants and the glass itself looks old to give a feeling that it has always been there. Mirrored panels on opening and closing doors add a nice touch: it is fascinating to see reflections at different angles.

Painted *trompe l'œil* panels are another way of suggesting more space. If you feel like having a go yourself and, like me, are not very experienced in the art, it is worth buying a book on the subject and practising where it does not matter. I would keep the colours light and subtle, even worn-out, to suggest a fresco. Any mistakes can then be hidden by a 'repair'! I think this kind of effect needs an element of fantasy or humour; make it fun. Finally, keep it to one panel and – as with the mirror – overgrow the sides with bold plants in pots to hide the join.

When making a garden it is easy to forget just how much can be improved with the planting. I once made a Venetian window out of trellis to relieve a blind end-wall. It looked a little raw at first but, after closely planted variegated ivy had established itself, it quickly achieved a look of maturity.

FAR LEFT *A light-hearted, mirrored arch teasingly lends another dimension to this little spring garden.*
MIDDLE LEFT *The sense of depth in a shaded path at Hidcote is enhanced by this series of arches, while the horizontally laid flagstones lead the eye to the sides of the walk.*
LEFT *I like the way this* trompe l'oeil *panel, set off by the bold antique arch, suggests a Mediterranean view; but if you preferred you could make it even softer, so that it begins to resemble an antique fresco.*

GENEROSITY OF FORM

Because nearly all town gardens are surrounded by buildings they can easily feel overwhelmed by the cityscape beyond. If the bones are weak, a place will never have that air of settled tranquillity essential to any beautiful garden. In a small garden, you need to make a visual impact to give your place its own strong character; when your garden is being crowded from all sides, you need something within it pushing out – something to redress the balance between the large space outside and the small one within.

The garden in the picture on the right belongs to an elegant eighteenth-century town house and needed sensitive handling. Any trick devices were out of the question and my only brief was that all the flowers I planted had to be white. I decided the best thing to do was to excavate a terrace and pave it in old bricks to match the house. Then, leading to the garden proper, I built a generous staircase running the entire width of the house to give the garden a sense of breadth. The width of the flight almost seems to push the narrow boundaries of the space apart.

Large, overscaled objects and generous architecture, rather than shrinking an outside space as you might expect, will suggest a bigger place to the eye. It is all a question of making the most of what you have already, or could have, within the space available. In this way, gardens are not so different from a stage set.

The surprisingly generous width of these steps makes the 'bones' of the garden stand up well against the large scale of the surrounding buildings. However, the staircase needed dressing to prevent its strength from feeling unfriendly. I decorated either side with cubes of clipped box and – one of my favourite devices – added stone balls echoing box balls in the border; so linking the stairs with the garden. Cotoneaster horizontalis *and* Soleirolia soleirolii *further soften the steps.*

Scale

The artificial environment of a roof is the perfect place to live out a few fantasies and let yourself go. It must be something to do with being away from the ground: in a conventional garden, people expect to see things growing out of the soil. Crazy paint colours and overt artificiality simply do not work at ground level unless in small, subtle doses. But two, ten or two hundred storeys up, anything goes.

Because of their often striking surroundings, roof gardens – whether the view is the sky or buildings – require strong architectural elements within their space to prevent them from being completely overwhelmed by their backdrop. If ever a site was crushed by buildings it was this one situated on the roof of a fashionable restaurant. Great cliffs of brick, stone and glass bore down on the narrow space, devouring nearly all the light.

Laying floors in chequered squares or rectangles always creates a feeling of space. At ground level these bright colours would look artificial, but here in this roof garden the black and white pattern adds sparkle to what is basically a sunless garden, while the raspberry and Chinese-yellow tubs add warmth.

The owners originally hankered after a hedge grown in troughs. But, as I pointed out, the view of the uncomfortably close skyscrapers needed to be broken up in an interesting way – with the movement and life that only plants can bring. Having made that decision, I knew that whatever shrubs or trees were chosen, they should not fight the backdrop of buildings, but enhance it by way of contrast.

Looking around for inspiration, and with no obvious lead, I started in the minimalist drawing room running the entire length of the balcony. Two sofas, one in raspberry and the other in Chinese-yellow silk, were the starting point. It is exciting to create a link between the house and the garden, softening the boundaries between inside and out. Four massive tubs were painted in matt-finish masonry paint, mixed to the exact colour of the sofas. Randomly placed along the balcony's perimeters, they were planted with enormous *Cordyline australis*. I added palms *(Trachycarpus fortunei)* and black bamboo in matt-black tubs to keep things varied.

Suddenly there was a garden. The cool, white limestone and brick interior came to life and the views from the windows, now seen through the decorative palm leaves, were, dare I say it, smart. Against the gruff buildings the palm's foliage was strong but elegant, whereas anything more delicate might have felt awkward.

LEFT AND ABOVE *Strong lines and colours prevent this garden from being overwhelmed by the high buildings that surround it. The bold plants, randomly placed, save it from any feeling of hardness while the height of the palms give it a sense of protectedness. The globes of box provide a moveable feast of pattern.*

PLANTING PLAN
3.5m/11ft wide × 9m/30ft long

❶ *Cordyline australis* in raspberry and Chinese-yellow tubs
❷ Different sized box balls *(Buxus sempervirens)* in pots
❸ Black bamboo *(Phyllostachys nigra)*
❹ Black and white painted floor
❺ *Fatsia japonica* in black tub
❻ Table and chairs
❼ *Trachycarpus fortunei* in black tub

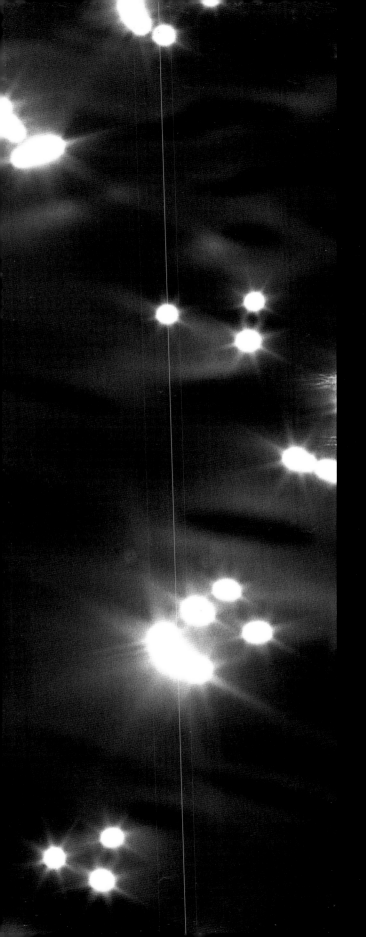

Water

& Light

Water offers so many possibilities: elegant formal pools or relaxed, natural ponds with abundant water planting; tumbling fountains or calm, looking-glass surfaces. The way you intend to use water will have so much influence on the way a garden comes together that I think it should be among the first things that you consider when you are planning it.

And if you have water in your garden, why not light it? Uplight a formal pool to create glimmering reflections, spotlight a detail or create sensational effects for a special occasion – the combination of water and light is magical.

PERFECT POOLS

Water, especially moving water, brings a small garden to life as nothing else can. The variety and style of features at your disposal are limited only by your imagination and ingenuity, but I would add that pools can look boring without the movement and life of a fountain.

In small gardens, it is possible to use water on a larger scale than you might at first imagine. Do not be afraid to make it the focus of your garden. Too many people add a mean-looking feature after everything else has been completed, when really a pool can be the heartbeat of a place. Overscale, and let the flourish of grander gardens inspire you.

In a temperate climate, try to place your fountain in a place where it will catch the sun for at least part of the day. If it is not lit the effect of the cold water can be chilly: few people will want to linger by a gloomy pool. Even a secluded ferny grotto should have the odd shaft of sunlight to bring it to life.

These days there are excellent fibreglass reproductions of lead and bronze water-tanks, urns and antique decorative pumps on the market. The best are almost indistinguishable from the real thing and require nothing more than water, a safe electrical connection (do appoint a qualified electrician!) and perhaps a few well-chosen plants. Alternatively, you could of course build a conventional pool. Actually they are much easier to build than you might imagine, almost maintenance-free and (like all things connected with gardens) remarkably good value.

The most modest wall-fountain will bring all the charm of a Provençal village square to your backyard. Water tumbling on to stone, or thrown into the air to explode into a thousand tiny stars, will take the most unsentimental person into another world.

ABOVE LEFT *The harmony and proportions of Achille Duchêne's water parterre at Blenheim provide inspiration for smaller gardens.*
ABOVE *Although this copper, tree-fantasy fountain is from a grand garden, Chatsworth, there is no reason why a small garden could not contain something similar.*
RIGHT *The contribution a pool such as this makes to a garden is easily worth its expense.*

FORMAL WATER

A formal pool is an opportunity to bring some real style and elegance to your garden. Your pool can be traditional or uncompromisingly modern, but the craftsmanship should be faultless, the lines geometric and the materials interesting. Formal pools need to be given pride of place in a scheme, but your garden really does not have to be large to use them.

The real beauty of a formal pool is the water itself and, even in the tiniest space, you can make the area covered by the water much larger than you imagine. Interestingly, expanses of water act like a looking-glass and can double the apparent size of your garden.

The more elaborate your pool, the simpler the surroundings should be – the play of the water as it tumbles on to the surface should be enough decoration in itself. In my opinion, formal pools are best left unplanted as clean, sweeping lines will develop the elegance you should be aiming for. If you are in any doubt about the size, always overscale; details can be added later.

LEFT The quiet elegance of this modern pool is set off by banks of flowers, while the dark backdrop lends the column focus.

ABOVE *The red marble panels and bronze dolphins of this pool remind me of a bathroom in some exotic palace.*
BELOW *I love the way these water spouts are set into sandy hieroglyphic panels.*

SECRET POOLS

BELOW *This old pump makes a charming detail where a more formal piece might be too severe. The contrasting leaves of the well-organized but informal planting make a strong yet somehow delicate setting for the magnificent old sink.*

On a warm summer evening when the garden is overgrown with flowers, what could be more delightful than to hear the murmur of running water in the background and to come upon a silver pool bringing a breath of the country into the garden?

In an informal pool, luxuriant water-planting gives a lovely feeling of not quite knowing where the land ends and the water begins. It is easy to get carried away with the bewildering variety of plants available to a water-gardener, though; much better to go with one or two favourites, let them grow, and then add the odd thing as and when you see it. Do leave some clear space in the centre of your pool – part of the beauty is seeing the surrounding plants reflected in the water.

Make a stepped pool so that you can grow some of the beautiful marginal plants: hostas, water irises and drumstick primulas *(Primula denticulata)*. Actually in the water, it would be lovely to contrast the water iris with ornamental rhubarb's ruddy cut leaves. American skunk cabbage *(Symplocarpus foetidus)* does best in marshy soil if you can give it the depth (0.75m/2½ft) it needs: this plant has one of the largest, most striking, matt olive-green leaves I have ever seen. If you can contrive to site your pool with plenty of plants behind, it will become doubly spectacular. If you had the room, you could complement a formal pool, with fountains *en fête*, with a quieter, lusher one tucked away in a corner.

RIGHT ABOVE *Romantic tumbles of white roses make this pool and fountain look as if they have always been there. The way the water plants are allowed full rein, while the containing lines of the brick paving draw the eye to the little pool, creates a nice contrast.*
RIGHT BELOW *The straight lines of this pool provide an elegant structure for the informal ornamental rhubarb* (Rheum palmatum 'Atrosanguineum') *in the foreground.*

MASKS

Masks provide that subtle, classic feel that so becomes a garden: a mask placed on a wall, especially if it feeds an elevated pool (perhaps a trough, stone sink or lead cistern), can be very dramatic – the first thing you notice as you enter the space. You can use masks (perhaps in groups) to strike either a formal or a more relaxed note; they work in either situation, bringing a spirit of generosity and antiquity reminiscent of grander, larger places.

The most successfully placed pool I have ever designed was a formal, raised one about 6m/20ft away from the house, opposite large French windows leading out into the garden. The garden itself was on the bare side: a classic combination of whitewashed trellis against shell-pink brick walls, an old flagstone floor; some antique figures and a couple of red-leaved trees underplanted with grey hostas in raised beds.

Nothing else was needed because the pool, with its formal, central mask, set against a rusticated chimney-breast, seemed to fill the garden. Everything was subservient to it – as to a grand fireplace in a room – and, with the fascination of the moving water falling into the pool below, you only noticed the rest of the place later.

As a struggling actor with little money, I recycled an old kitchen sink and a discarded lion's head mask to make a less formal feature for my first garden (see right). The mask had been damaged and roughly repaired and, as I chipped the glaze from the sink, I found that in quite a short time I had something that easily passed for stone. I then filled it with rocks and cobbles. Set into the garden wall, with no attempt to hide the repairs and surrounded by fast-growing golden hop, it soon developed a look of antiquity. I hid the mechanics – a small sunken reservoir and pump – behind striped pots containing box balls.

LEFT *The repaired lion's head spouts water into the 'stone' trough, formerly a kitchen sink, in my first garden. I am very fond of this lion; he has a most benevolent expression. With any statuary, it is important that you actually like their characters!*

ABOVE *With three lions' heads, this pool has generosity, luxury and that most desirable garden quality – surprise. The miraculously slim, architectural papyrus, their huge umbels gracefully hovering above, strikes just the right note of lightness.*

STARTLING REFLECTIONS

When using lighting in a garden, especially near water, you have to remember the golden rule that I learned in the theatre: many small light-sources are better than a few large ones. Once the cables are laid, the expense of extra fittings is negligible, so be generous.

Overhead lighting can be disastrous with water. Reflections dazzle visitors, the floor of the pond can be illuminated and, horror of horrors, the actual fitting may be reflected in the water for all the world to see! Outside lighting should be magical, and therefore invisible. With a formal pool you should certainly use uplighting under the water itself. Uplighters are glamorous anyway, but add water and the effect takes on a whole new dimension – the glimmering reflections are incredible.

When it comes to lighting an informal, or planted, pool, I would go for tiny, adjustable fittings on spikes in the ground – near the water rather than in it. Aim them to uplight or side-light the plants, and the reflections will be stunning. If you use underwater fittings in an informal setting, you run the risk of showing up plant baskets, supporting bricks, roots or any other old thing that happens to be in the water.

Most importantly, lighting near water must be safe. Use low-voltage halogen lights and insist on a power-breaker. Experiment, but enjoy it.

LEFT *Understated in its elegance, this fountain sparkles subtly during the day; then at night, when the chic panels of clipped climbing plants have become no more than a suggestion the uplit fountain comes into its own – a perfect detail in a modern scene.* RIGHT *The gentle gleam of underwater uplighting transforms this formal pool.*

41

WHEN THE LIGHTS ARE LOW

So few of us use our gardens at night. It seems a waste for, like sunny days, warm evenings are not – even in a temperate climate – a rare occurrence. I long for an exterior fireplace under a loggia; meanwhile I can think of nothing nicer than an evening in the garden with good company, in which scented flowers and subtle lighting transport my guests and me to wherever we wanted to be.

It is true that the lower the lights are placed, the more flattering to people, spaces and objects they are. You can hide tiny, low-voltage spots behind box balls punctuating the front of a border or, perhaps, behind large pots. Both would throw the shapes into interesting relief. Urns, in particular, look great uplit; fittings cut into stone paving slabs (protected by stainless-steel portholes) make the urns above appear to float.

I have a weakness for decorative lanterns. Good eighteenth- or nineteenth-century reproductions, once repainted in black or darkest green gloss (as gloss-finish paint shows up, rather than hides, brush-marks) to cover up the manufacturer's somewhat soulless spray-paint finish, are indistinguishable from the real thing. If the light-bulb is visible, make sure you use a clear glass one, preferably in a plain candle shape. Avoid twists and artful 'realistic flames' at all costs!

Generally though, all permanent light fittings, except those that double as decoration, should be well hidden from view.

ABOVE *As the sun goes down, these 'three graces' come into their own as a generous circle of uplighters bathes them in light.*
RIGHT *I knew when I designed this little garden – with entertaining in mind – that, once lit, simplicity would be more telling than something more complicated. The lighting is a balance of eyeball spotlights (strategically hidden in the ivy-covered walls) and adjustable uplighters.*

LIGHTING FOR SPECIAL OCCASIONS

Lighting for a special occasion is quite a different thing from permanent outside lighting. Flares, candles and night-lights cannot draw specific attention to a specific feature, but they do softly highlight an area, rather like decorative lanterns. If your temporary lighting is too serious, you are missing the point: it should be frivolous and fun.

I have seen a garden with a broad path leading to the front door that, just for the evening, the owners had turned into a walk of lights. With nothing more than night-lights in jam-jars every couple of steps along the path, it looked welcoming and glamorous.

It does not matter if your fixtures do not look particularly professional – if, say, the jam-jars are all slightly different. The surprise of seeing lighting on a special occasion, and the fact that somebody has gone to the trouble of arranging it, is welcoming in itself. Really, after dark you will notice only the little flames or fairy lights anyway.

LEFT *With the candles in flower pots, it is as if this rather theatrical garden is dressed for a party. The candles make the garden welcoming and, along with the gnarled branches of the tree, create a grotto-like effect; a magical wonderland.*
RIGHT ABOVE *Fairy lights flung through the branches of trees have a simple childlike appeal and lend this corner of the garden an air of secrecy.*
RIGHT *This garden table, overflowing with multicoloured candles and flowers, would make a charming setting for an evening with old friends.*

for a Star

As the shadows lengthen, and one by one the stars appear, good lighting in your garden can whisk you into an enchanted new world. Anything is possible. A tree, figure or group of flowers barely noticed by day suddenly takes on all the magic of the theatre as neighbouring distractions drift away into the night. Here, I was able to turn a small, scented space into what its owner describes as 'a little Wagnerian opera set'.

Water and lighting are two of the most exciting things you can give your garden, yet many people feel they are beyond them. 'Too luxurious,' they say, 'all we want is a place to sit, and a few flowers.' While I sympathize, I feel it is a shame. For very little time, trouble and expense, these two elements bring glamour and romance to the smallest space.

In this garden, each urn is bathed in light by uplighters set into the paving, while the pool is lit from underwater. As the fountains play, hundreds of golden spangles are thrown into the air. Magic! Everything else is uplit, with the exception of the main group of Versailles tubs on the steps, which have

Urns placed down the sides of this garden break up the long lines of the boundaries, while smaller urns on the 'chimney-piece' take up the theme. Behind the chimney-piece, on a slightly higher level, is a secret garden. The uplighting creates a satisfying effect of light and shadow with the different shapes of the urns, spiky palms and soft, dense box.

their own eyeball spotlight set high on the house. The whole system is on dimmers, so the mood can be controlled at the flick of a switch – high for full dramatic effect or low for dinner under the stars.

By day, however lovely the flowers and plants, all gardens, like rooms, need something extra to set them alight. And nothing is as fascinating as the movement and sparkle of water playing in a fountain.

Decorators tell us that rooms will look larger if the furniture is placed against the walls. The same is true in gardens, especially small ones (which I often think of as rooms without ceilings). This is where wall-backed fountains come into their own. They have a nice architectural feel and are economical on space; when cleverly placed, they can provide a focal point for an extra axis or dimension. Here, I raised the fountain to harmonize with the flight of steps near the house, but the surrounding ledge of a elevated pool also makes a pleasant place to sit on a hot summer's day – and a good spot

to place moisture-loving plants such as hydrangeas.

As I placed the wall-backed pool three-quarters of the way up the garden, there was room for a small secret garden behind it. This gravel courtyard is the perfect place to enjoy a pre-dinner drink. Apart from the old tree and wrought iron benches, two partying cherubs provide the only decoration here. I lit the small area simply by uplighting the cherubs, concealing the fittings in glass and stainless steel portholes set into the gravel. These spotlights are directly in front of the figures to accentuate their beauty; if the light source was behind, or to the side, the effect would create an interesting silhouette, but without much of the detail.

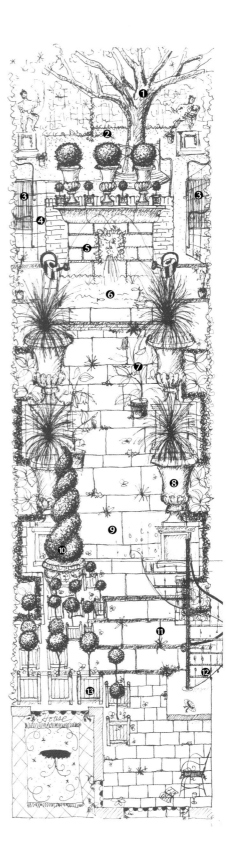

GARDEN PLAN 5m/17ft wide × 27.5m/90ft long

❶ Sycamore tree with wisteria growing through the branches

❷ Secret gravel garden

❸ Benches

❹ Gate in trellis, partly concealed by a 'chimney-breast'-style wall with stone balls along the top

❺ Lion's mask fountain

❻ Formal pool

❼ Planting in containers, changes seasonally

❽ 2.1m/7ft urns, planted with cordylines (**Cordyline australis**)

❾ Flagstones laid in horizontal bands

❿ 2.1m/7ft box spiral, in terracotta pot

⓫ Shallow flight of four steps

⓬ Spiral staircase to a balcony above

⓭ Versailles containers on the steps, planted with seasonal flowers and mop-head box trees (**Buxus sempervirens**)

ABOVE *Lit from below, at night the flowing lines of the figure of a cherub make a nice contrast with the squared trellis. The details of the statue gently gleam, accentuated by lights in front.*

LEFT *As the fountains play, an underwater light source, placed directly beneath the water jet, catches the droplets and casts wonderful reflections all around the garden.*

Soft
is best

Gardens ought to feel as if they have been there for ever. It was on an early visit to Sissinghurst, where I saw erysimum in the ancient moat wall thriving on a diet of nothing more than old mortar, that I first realized the importance of the patina of time. Too often, gardens look as if they have been there for twenty minutes rather than twenty years.

Watching moss and lichen slowly developing over stone and brick gives me as much pleasure as almost anything else in the garden. But you do not have to wait for time to bring these softening effects: using faux antiques, carefully choosing paving materials and inserting creeping plants between stones are all among the tricks that will hasten that timeless look.

ETERNAL CHARM

There is no getting away from the fact that a brand-new garden is not a very attractive place to be in. Hopeful, yes; attractive, no. Gardens need to feel settled if they are to refresh your spirit and, before any fun decoration or paint effects begin, you need to have that well-established look to avoid it appearing hard and brash. I am often concerned with making a garden look as if it has been there for a long while in the shortest possible time. Do not despair; there are short cuts.

You do not always need antiques in your garden. There are a few (bits of decorative masonry, old watering-cans and hand-made pots are ones I can think of) that I would not be without, but I often prefer good reproduction ornaments and furniture; then I at least know they will not collapse. My garden antiques are now box and yew topiaries, which, as I clip them, are becoming more and more velvety – they will move house when I do.

The most important point is that there has to be a solidity about a place. Often the sheer size of an object can suggest antiquity. You know that it could not just be picked up with one hand or whipped away in a summer gale. If in doubt, always overscale – it is easy to say, but it does take some courage to do. Once placed, however imposing a large object might look to begin with, it will become more and more beautiful.

I am not suggesting that everything should be fake olde-worldy, just that a garden should look settled; once in place, you can add fun touches. A garden needs a balance between the two.

LEFT *The gentleness of a weathered finish on garden furniture and ornament works to suggest great age. Oak weathers to a beautiful silver colour. This Queen Anne-style corner settle would not look half as lovely if it were painted, even in the most beautiful colour imaginable.*

BELOW *You cannot help wondering how many hundreds of years this solid-looking bench has been in place. The background is also superb and warms up the cool old stone. Bench, wall and floor create the sort of effect that looks as though it took centuries to achieve.*

PAVING THE WAY

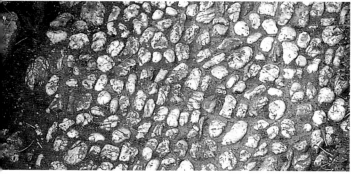

ABOVE (FROM TOP) *Brick, especially when aged by moss and lichen growing in between, is the most pleasing of pavings although cobbles have a rough, informal feel and work particularly well near water. Herring-bone can look good in wide expanses, but often looks best as narrow paths between box hedges.*
RIGHT *It is not always practical to use old York stone. This picture shows how you can dress it up with that most useful plant, Soleirolia soleirolii.*

In an ideal world, we would all have rooms covered in acres of Persian carpet or miles of finest parquet (polished by somebody else!). Outside, nothing is lovelier than old stone and ancient brick: the handsome effect is easily worth the expense and effort.

The best investment I ever made was to pave my garden. Admittedly I went for the best and chose old York stone, but the timeless beauty of the material is so great that it was worth every penny. Apart from the odd sweep of a brush it is maintenance-free and, by using one extra-large piece as a shallow step, I was even able to introduce a change in level to lend variation and a feeling of quality to what is basically a flat site.

I like both brick and stone to be laid simply on well-prepared and levelled earth, or earth and sand, closely butted up with plants in between. Not only are paths easier to lay without pointing, but the gaps allow moss and lichen to develop slowly between the slabs. I paint the surfaces with milk, yoghurt and soil to further encourage the feeling of antiquity.

If your house is built of brick, use it for your hard surfaces too. In fact whatever your house is made of, you cannot go wrong with brick paving. Some people prefer bricks laid on edge (for a fine, detailed effect). However, I like to see them laid flat, especially in small spaces, for several reasons: the bigger face contrasts subtly with the slimmer edge seen in the house walls, while the larger scale of the face is less overwhelmed by any surrounding buildings; this larger scale also makes for a smoother transition when brick meets stone; and, finally, it is easier and less expensive – you need fewer bricks!

Bricks laid in a basket-weave pattern are pretty, and I think that herring-bone pattern paths are particularly charming. Cobbles can make an interesting change – used, for instance, surrounding an old sink. Gravel is easy and inexpensive, but is best kept well away from the house – think of those carpets!

PLANTS FOR FLOORS

It is one of the great untold truths of gardening that nearly all plants love to get their roots securely under stone. It is a perfect environment for them – never too wet and never too dry. Once your soft, mossy paving is in place, you can start to think about planting. This business of pavement gardening is so delightful, that when I lay stone, I concentrate on getting the edges in line and do not worry about any gaps between the slabs – the more there are, the more plants I can fit in.

There are no rules; it is limited only by your imagination. All you need is something to kneel on, a trowel, an old kitchen knife and a little grit and potting compost to help the plants get established.

The sunny areas are the easiest. Dibble in creeping thyme (some of the tiny ones such as *Thymus serpyllum* do not mind being walked on), foaming rock roses, saxifrage, wall daisies (*Erigeron karvinskianus*), thrift – the white (*Armeria maritima* 'Alba') and soft terracotta (*Armeria maritima* 'Corsica') varieties are prettiest – any little thing as and when you see it.

Around the edges, you could start with hundreds of snowdrops in early spring, both single and double. They like to be buried deep (8-10 cm/3-4 in), and should be planted in the green (with the leaves still intact). Try not to separate the clumps and plant in masses of no fewer than ten; be generous. Once established they will be with you for life, flowering more and more generously with each spring.

Still in the sun, especially around the margins, grey-leaved lavender, rosemary or *Melianthus* bring elegance and structure. In the shade, silver painted ferns, scented daphne, pansies, primulas, the tiny creeping mint, soleirolia . . . is that enough?

But try it yourself, it is so easy. And who knows? You may wake up one spring morning and find your paving has turned itself into something as pretty as Botticelli's *Primavera*.

FAR LEFT *The coral flowers of this rock rose* (Helianthemum) *set against old stone look stunning. The mellow lichened texture of the terracotta in the background is exceptional too; you could try the effect with a pot overflowing with soft yellow or cream flowers.*

ABOVE LEFT Cerastium tomentosum *is pretty and useful where it can have its fling untamed, although it can be rather a thug.* C. columnae *is less invasive but just as pretty.*

BELOW LEFT *When we were children, we were fascinated by the house leeks* (Sempervivum tectorum) *that grew on the roof of our old farm house. In a hot summer, they would send out several exotic-looking flowers. It will grow on a vertical surface, but here they squeeze into a crack and break up a hard line.*

PLANTS FOR WALLS

ABOVE Rosa *'Guinée'*
is beautifully set off by
the old stone wall. The
trellis has almost been
designer colour-matched!
RIGHT *Romantically*
overgrown with old
roses, this beautiful arch
is pervaded with the air
of nostalgie du temps
perdu. *The creamy*
flowers of Rosa
'Leverkusen' look great
against this crumbling
old wall and the old
pantiled roof beyond
offers a change of
texture.

Remember that the walls of your house are part of the garden, and climbers can disguise the most ordinary, or even ugly, architecture. House walls, after all, have two sides and why should interiors have all the fun?

In the absence of old walls I use panels of trellis to grow plants up. If you need more seclusion, back the trellis with ordinary close-boarded fencing. After you have established your boundaries, begin to soften them with climbers like variegated ivy and golden hop (*Humulus lupulus* 'Aureus').

Should you be lucky enough to have an old garden wall, carefully tap out the odd hole in the mortar (at eye level looks nice) and gently squeeze in an aubrieta, house-leek (*Sempervivum*) or *Erigeron karvinskianus*. I particularly like erigeron's clouds of tiny pink and white daisies: it will seed everywhere but never become a nuisance.

Even a shady wall will support all sorts of lovely things – roses and clematis: *Rosa* 'Mermaid', whose soft-yellow, single flowers combine beautifully with the dark *Clematis* 'Etoile Violette'; and *Rosa* 'Madame Alfred Carrière's white flowers suffused with palest pink are marvellous with *Clematis* 'Etoile Rose', an expensive-looking soft pink. All the honeysuckles are good in the shade too – try the grey-leaved, yellow-flowered *Lonicera tragophylla* with the claret-coloured *Clematis* 'Niobe'. Wherever possible, train a climber along horizontal wires on the wall or fence as will you get more flowers that way .

The subject of climbers is so vast that it requires books (of which there are many) to itself – I have discussed some more on page 94. However you decide to soften and decorate the walls of your garden is, like your sitting room, down to personal taste. But I would add that not taking full advantage of climbers should be made a criminal offence: give them plenty of room and those fragile sticks from the nursery will amaze you.

SOFT POTS

Terracotta pots look so much better old than new. In no time at all you can make them evocative of a Renaissance *palazzo* or a Tuscan terrace. It is fun to do and the results are well worth it.

When reproduction or modern pots arrive, the first thing I do (after planting them) is to soften the rims and protruding mouldings with a light sanding using the coarsest paper I can find. Next, starting at the top, I carefully dribble diluted white, cream or pale-grey paint (it does not matter whether it is masonry paint, emulsion or egg-shell – but avoid gloss) down the sides here and there, to suggest lime encrustation.

The next day, I pour milk over the entire surface. Then, while it is still tacky, I rub in earth or any compost I might have around using old gardening gloves. To really get the algae going, rub weeds or discarded plants below the mouldings; the green of the plants does not run off in the rain and looks very realistic. The damper you keep the pot, the more quickly moss and lichen develop so, when you water the plant, water the pot's exterior as well – occasionally allowing the muddy water to overflow. Commercial liquid manure rubbed into the surface neat, or dribbled down the edges in dilute form also encourages organic growth, as do cow manure and water, live yoghurt and urine.

Some of the most beautiful garden objects I have seen are antique amphorae. Made in Mediterranean countries to store wine or olive oil, these pots often remained in the same family for hundreds of years, and were repainted each spring. As the elements gradually wear down these successive coats of paint, a chalky patina develops; you can re-create this look by applying some of the lovely water-based powder paints available to the main part of the pot. Do this in a rustic manner – applying, perhaps, a white coat followed by ones of pastel green and blue. Then gently sand down to reveal the different layers.

LEFT *It is not only the powerful presence of this pot that makes it remarkable, but the surface too. Coat upon coat of waterbased paint has gradually flaked away to leave a delicate texture. You could re-create the effect on any terracotta pot by painting it with old-fashioned distemper paint and gently sanding it down.*
ABOVE RIGHT *The chalky texture of this amphora is complemented by its elegant shape. Really, to be safe, it should be standing on a simple iron stand. You can buy old pots like this, but it is almost more fun to try and achieve the effect yourself, again painting a pot with distemper paint and sanding it down.*
RIGHT *A lichen effect like this can be achieved in many ways, such as painting on watered-down manure, milk or live yoghurt.*

Chic

I first saw this garden on a winter's afternoon just after the bricks had been laid. The builders had barely finished and, as a brand new garden does, it all felt very cold – a feeling not helped by the weather. On the other hand, it was an exciting challenge to have a bare canvas on which to work. I could hardly wait to get started. Walking round the site, I knew that the most important thing was to make the garden look lived in and friendly – it needed furnishing and softening.

Unrestored antique French table and chairs complete the picture here, but what really gives the whole garden soul is the mossy overgrown floor. It is hard to believe that the romantic-looking surface in these pictures originally filled me with despair. Although well-laid in a herring-bone pattern, the wide expanse of pink, industrial brick looked hard and cold. To me it had all the romance of a cinema boiler-house backing on to a car park and it badly needed some soul. Now, however, the bright emerald green of the *Soleirolia soleirolii* is astonishingly beautiful. It is also maintenance-free and cost next to nothing.

Soleirolia soleirolii *loves to grow in the cracks between stone and brick. This useful plant will soften anything you like and put up with a considerable amount of shade. For the deepest emerald colour, feed it occasionally with a granular fertilizer, especially just before some rain or a shower from the hose.*

Using sledge-hammers we broke the bricks up, then scattered the surface with earth and lightly planted it all over with sprigs of soleirolia. Apart from a daily sprinkle of the hose while it was getting established, nature did the rest.

The garden already had a strong focus: a centrally placed pool abutting the far wall. This pool was fed by a specially commissioned lion's head fountain that I felt looked a little hard. Set at eye-level it looked too blatant and altogether too dramatic so I took a hammer to it and managed to 'smooth' some of its lines to give it a look of antiquity.

The pool's centrality on the back wall meant everything else had to be symmetrical. I started by flanking it with a pair of flowering crab apple trees. These are perfect for town gardens as their canopy of branches is so light and, to me, their flowers are more delicate than a flowering cherry's. Besides adding height, they softly framed the pond and simultaneously smudged what had been the rather hard outline of the back wall.

Two stone benches either side of the garden were enclosed by azure-blue and white striped tubs containing box mop-heads and seasonal flowers. Scattered around each were clusters of old flowerpots planted with box balls, again to smudge any long lines. Next, I developed a sense of enclosure with box-edged borders either side of the steps near the house. These were set with metal obelisks supporting *Rosa* 'Zigeunerknabe' and underplanted with black-leaved *Ophiopogon planiscapus* 'Nigrescens' (a very long name for an easy-going, effective plant).

As a backdrop to the pool, trellis walls covered in grey and green variegated ivy *(Hedera canariensis* 'Gloire de Marengo') bring year-round privacy and, together with the flowering crab trees, make a delightful but simple, soft ending to the garden.

The plants in this paving give the illusion of a lawn where grass would never grow, creating a soft effect that is easy to maintain. The ivy-clad walls, box hedges and twists all give freshness which is enhanced by the summer planting of Danish marguerites and the striped pots.

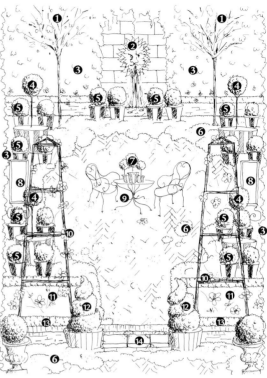

❶ *Malus* 'Golden Hornet'

❷ Lion's mask fountain

❸ *Hedera canariensis* 'Gloire de Marengo'

❹ Box mop-heads *(Buxus sempervirens)*

❺ Pairs of box balls in black and white pots

❻ *Soleirolia soleirolii* on distressed bricks

❼ Miniature box mop-heads

❽ Stone benches

❾ Antique French chairs and table in original
   white paint

❿ *Rosa* 'Zigeunerknabe' on emerald painted metal
   obelisks

⓫ Black-leaved *Ophiopogon planiscapus*
   'Nigrescens'

⓬ Box spirals *(Buxus sempervirens)*

⓭ Box hedging *(Buxus sempervirens)*

⓮ Stone step

The **Art**
of Decoration

I love decoration, and have even been described as a decorator-gardener. Flattering or disparaging as that may be, it seems to me that when the spaces you work on are often not much bigger than the average room, you cannot afford to ignore the possibilities that decorative effects offer. Using colour and features to make the most of walls, livening up windowsills, adding decorative detail, and choosing stylish seating and containers can make all the difference to the tiniest of garden spaces. Perhaps more people should aspire to become decorator-gardeners!

BACKGROUND COLOUR

I have always hankered after an all-white drawing room but, for me, white has never worked as a colourwash on a wall outside. I find it rather cold and unflattering to plants, and it is not the answer to a dingy corner where the sun never shines. In hot climates, white looks wonderful, but where the weather is more temperate, unless you live in a clapper-boarded house or perhaps near the sea, I would avoid white walls – in the shade they look too cold, and in the sun they glare.

It all depends on the light, but as a general rule of thumb I have found the natural shell-pink known as Fowler Pink (after the distinguished interior designer John Fowler, of Colefax and Fowler) cannot be bettered. On a north wall it gently warms a drab aspect and there are few plants that are not complemented by the colour's soft background.

I am a great fan of these heritage or historical paints; they are made using traditional ingredients such as lampblack and, while they are more expensive than something more chemical-looking, you cannot go wrong with them. They are ideal in the garden as they blend well with plants. Never worry about paint fading or peeling – it will add to the charm.

RIGHT *Walls painted in Fowler Pink are the next best thing to a background of warm honeyed stone or soft Tudor bricks. Like stone or brick, the colour makes a sympathetic setting for almost any plant.*
LEFT *A classic colour scheme of darkest green and warm cream. And even the curtains are right.*

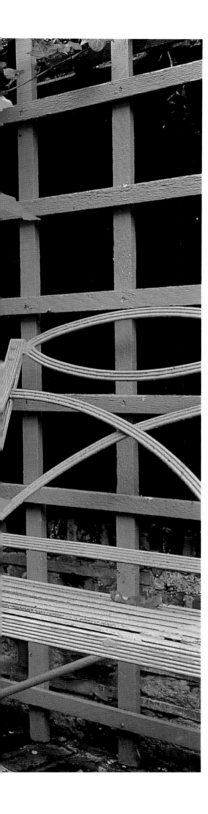

ALL FOR WALLS

The whole point about wall features – whether actually against walls, hedges or trellis – is that they should look relaxed, having a certain inevitability.

A lead cherub against a trellised wall works well, because the square lines of the trellis contrast with the rococo lines of the figure without being overpowering. Painting the wall behind the same green as the trellis keeps everything subtle. Groups of stone balls topping walls of the same material are used to great effect at Chiswick House in London, lending interest to what might otherwise be a boring profile and creating dramatic shadows. I am not too proud to reveal that I copied this idea for the wall outside my own back door, using reconstituted stone balls softened with wall plants.

Another idea from the past is to place metal urns on top of a wall and paint them a very dark green. They do not need to be vast in size, and inexpensive modern copies are almost indistinguishable from antiques. Alternatively, larger matt-black urns or reconstituted stone pineapples on the piers either side of a gate look fantastic – and the higher they are placed, the better they look.

Doors can be enhanced with a cherub's head or a decorative lantern, placed either above or to one side, while entrances always benefit from being framed – by a pair of chairs or perhaps standard bay trees in tubs. Trellis can be decorative in its own right, especially in a place where few plants will grow: in the shade of a porch or under a balcony. Decorating walls is like wearing jewellery – too much and the effect will be lost. So go for a subtle effect, trying to enhance one particular feature and keeping it in scale with its surroundings.

LEFT *An exquisite eighteenth-century partying cherub is flattered by pea green paint. Without the modification of the trellis, the black background to the right would have been too strong for the delicacy of the piece.*
ABOVE *The deep terracotta wall finish and the soft pearl grey of the circular moulded frame combine to make a scene reminiscent of a Venetian garden. When the wisteria begins to flower, whether it is in lilac or white, the effect will be enhanced.*

WONDERFUL WINDOWSILLS

When you are dreaming at the window over a first cup of tea, your garden becomes a stage set, the window frame the proscenium arch and the line of box balls on your sill the footlights. Being greeted every morning by little balls of box peering in through the window is one of the nicest ways to start the day; they look great from the outside as well. Mine are planted in terracotta pots nearly the same colour as the walls of

LEFT Pelargonium *'Lord Bute' in an ordinary modern pot is given a lift by this experimental paint effect – my first!*

the house and, with a dark-green scalloped pelmet decorating the top of what was an indifferent window, they make a charming picture. I can hardly wait for the white *Rosa* 'Madame Alfred Carrière' to begin to soften the edges of the window frame.

In a garden setting, rows of small terracotta pots, or indeed any other containers, are much lighter in spirit than one solid window box: they have a quirkiness and rhythm that a single, solid container lacks. It is much better to keep boxes for windows facing the street. Lines of small containers pressing against the window are also an opportunity to echo larger versions in the garden beyond.

Miniature box topiaries are an excellent way of bringing charm to a sunless windowsill. Although they will grow in the sun with constant watering, the vigour of the plant is greater in the shade. Cyclamen, primulas, pansies, tobacco flowers and busy lizzies – I think the double ones are the prettiest – all do well on a shady windowsill.

In the sun, of course, you can grow almost anything. I would particularly recommend pelargoniums and petunias: both relish the protection of the house.

ABOVE Cyclamen persicum *in miniature Versailles tubs. They hardly ever need watering and put up with a considerable amount of shade.*
LEFT *A line of pots creates a lighter effect than a solid window box.*

DECORATIVE DETAILS

Details are crucial. How often has one looked at a superficially beautiful room, stage set or garden, only to find a disappointingly cheap-looking or historically incorrect touch, the one bad egg that spoils the cake.

I have always loved both architectural and decorative details. This was brought home to me when I was creating my new garden. Everything was in place and the main planting was done, but it did not feel like home until I had replaced the utilitarian handles on the garden door with antique ones found in a junk-shop. It all sounds rather precious, I suppose, but believe me, these things really do make all the difference.

While you sit in your garden on a warm summer's night, cast your eye over the various features. Could the profile of your (hopefully creeper-clad) shed be improved by a weathervane, your fence posts be made glamorous by some decoratively turned finials? Or how about building plinths to support a pair of stone pineapples? As I never tire of saying (I just have to hope nobody else tires of hearing it), all these things are much less expensive to do than you might think.

The moral of the story is: do not despise everyday garden objects. Old galvanized watering-cans, a rampant lion gracing a tiny windowsill, antique garden tools and even fragments of sculpture all add atmosphere. It is so easy and so effective – all it requires is a little planning and research.

TOP RIGHT *People are apt to forget the view above their heads. A weathervane like this proud cockerel would lift the most indifferent shed. Or you could even try a pennant, as on a medieval jousting tent.*
BOTTOM RIGHT *Bold decorative finials topping supporting posts turn an ordinary close-boarded fence into something with far higher aspirations – especially if the fence is adorned with trellis panels.*
FAR RIGHT *An inexpensive reproduction bought on a whim. Pastiche she may be, but she is beautiful in her setting of box and lilies.*

SEATING ARRANGEMENTS

Chairs and benches are a strong and evocative way to stamp your style on a garden – even an ultra-modern room can be enhanced by the elegant lines of a pair of Louis XVI armchairs. There are two elements you should remember when choosing chairs and benches: curves and colour.

I think curves are particularly effective because they contrast with paved surfaces while a garden is growing and, once it has settled, they blend nicely with the surrounding plants. Also, seats with flowing curves always look welcoming and comfortable: you want to sit on them.

It is so easy to change the colour of a seat that I used to do it four times a year – using cans of spray paint – just for fun: lime-yellow lightly oversprayed with matt black for the spring; a smart coat of turquoise lined with emerald in the summer; shocking pink for the autumn, surrounded by matt-black pots crammed with my favourite pink-centred, tiny white *Cyclamen persicum*; then red oversprayed with gold for a festive feeling at Christmas.

I am having a rest from bright colour until my new garden has grown. I feel you cannot play about like this until you have a well-founded backdrop; it works only when everything else is well covered in foliage and, even then, remember that paint should enhance, not dominate.

Ultimately benches and chairs should look as if they would be reasonably comfortable – or, if not, they should be so exquisitely elegant as to justify a place in any garden.

RIGHT *This Regency bench, elegant enough to have belonged to Beau Brummel, would lend style to the smallest space, and there would still be room for plants, even underneath. In this silver and pink setting, white is the only colour for it.*
BELOW *Unashamedly theatrical, this bench looks as if it belongs to an eighteenth-century landscape garden or the haunted ballroom scene in* Swan Lake. *In fact, it would sit with aplomb in almost any garden, yard or terrace.*

LEFT *Pure Paris, or is it Antibes? Their elegance apart, these little Matisse-style chairs are a great asset, light and easy to move around. They would also look charming painted darkest green with red and white checked cushions or, alternatively, smoky blue with blue and white cushions.*

TOP RIGHT *These useful folding chairs — this one smartly set against an informal planting including hydrangeas and hostas — can be stored in a cupboard and brought out for extra guests. I have a collection of them and each one is painted in a different colour. A design classic: everyone should have a few at least.*

MIDDLE RIGHT *These elegant campaign-style stools, distinguished by their graceful lines, look great as a pair. They would be even better in black and white striped canvas or linen and, if they were mine, they would definitely be covered in (amazingly historically correct) faux leopard skin.*

BOTTOM RIGHT *This turn-of-the-century American chair is actually a museum piece. I used to change its colour with the seasons but when I left my last garden I gave it away. Imagine my delight when I found identical casts at my favourite garden centre six months later.*

POTS OF STYLE

Containers are a heaven-sent opportunity to bring glamour, elegance and interest to the smallest setting. Broadly speaking, they fall into two categories: large pots – such as urns, swag-pots and Versailles tubs – that are permanently part of the garden's design; and smaller versions that you can move around.

Large containers are basically decorative architecture – perfect for small gardens. They can close a vista, flank a walk or even provide a strong foreground accent to stand against surrounding buildings. Like trellis pyramids, they lend height and structure where a tree would be too oppressive; they are also evocative of grander places. You can play them up or down according to your fancy, but do not worry about their grandeur; if your garden is surrounded by buildings they give it character and a sense of place.

In the first place urns and swag-pots have to be beautiful. Go for simplicity and elegance of shape on a solid-looking

plinth. Remember that, like paving and bricks, architectural urns have to look old and slightly crumbling to bring a breath of romance. If they look too new, the effect will be obtrusive. I carefully chip bits off with a hammer and pour milk all over, then rub in earth or discarded annuals. In a surprisingly short time, you have something that passes for a venerable antique.

In my experience, large statuary with strong flowers is too rich a combination for small gardens. Big urns, swag-pots and Versailles tubs, however – because of their simple, strong shapes – enhance the surrounding plants rather than attempting to upstage them. They demand simple planting to match. *Cordyline australis* 'Torbay Dazzler' or *Agave americana* 'Mediopicta Alba' in grey and white stripes take the spotlight well, as do *Astelia nervosa* or *A. chathamica*, an elegantly tattered

silken, silver flag. All are easy to grow as long as they have sun and sharp drainage.

Variations in both scale and material are important, but in moderation. Smaller containers let you show off a specific part of the garden for fun. Try to develop a stock of old pots for uses such as this; they are still around at reasonable prices. I treasure mine, and over the years have built up quite a little collection that ranges from low saucer shapes and square unglazed dishes to old strawberry planters and rhubarb-forcers that you turn upside down to use the top as your base.

I am wary of most metal containers except in special, mainly ultra-modern, situations. I do not much like to see rust as, often, instead of looking ancient it just looks shabby. There is a difference. An urn, Versailles tub or swag-pot, be it miniature or full size, should look beautifully cared for, but settled – like a cherished piece of furniture.

FAR LEFT *Inspired by Russian domes, the malachite paint effect of this urn really looks at its best in the winter. You could combine it with similar urns of distressed gold.*
LEFT *When space is limited, a well proportioned reproduction stone urn has a powerful presence. Simply planted with variegated* Cordyline australis *'Torbay Dazzler', it works well, whereas trailing plants would overcomplicate it.*
BELOW LEFT *A combination of grandeur and simplicity can look great. The galvanized florist's bucket contrasts with the swag-pot, while the rustic cabbages beneath the box ball set off the pure luxury of white lilies.*
BELOW RIGHT *A good urn this, permanently furnished with a clipped box pineapple and with bulbs for the spring.*

LEFT *Ranunculus are a neglected flower for early spring. They remind me of out-of-season peonies and I love them. The best colours are white, pale pink and deep pink; there is an orange variety that I do not care for. The soft green of the miniature Versailles tub makes a pleasant contrast with the darker box ball behind.*

BOTTOM LEFT *This Versailles tub is one of a double row of six. To avoid monotony, they were alternately painted in soft blue and cream. Formally grouped, their generosity can bring instant style to any terrace or paved area. I like them best planted with mop-heads of box surrounded by one variety of plant, but here the small-leaved helichrysum adds a soft, light touch.*

RIGHT *I had thought of repainting this 1950s jardinière that I found in a Brighton junk-shop, but when I got it home I found it was just right for the sumptuous little flowers of Viola 'Molly Sanderson'. These violas are amazing little plants: with deadheading and plenty of water, they will delight you throughout the summer.*

RIGHT *Here is an interesting departure. Effortlessly chic – and low-maintenance – these stainless-steel containers are excellent in the right setting. Not in one of my usual gardens on the ground, but terrific in a modern roof garden in the centre of town; or I can see them on a decking terrace overlooking the sea.*

BOTTOM RIGHT *One of these days, I will save up enough money to buy a genuine antique lead cistern. Highly decorative with its strapwork panel, this one with its understated topiary planting could not be bettered. It would look wonderful frosted with snow.*

LEFT *Checked pots look appalling if you try to paint them with masking tape as a guide; come to that, so do striped ones. Freehand stripes are much more in spirit with the natural terracotta. Here ordinary twigs sprayed with car spray-paint give a convincing impression of dogwood stems.*

LEFT *Here is a fun way to decorate a staircase. Repeated pots build their own rhythm and give a garden a gentle liveliness. These cycas palms, despite their appearance, are not desert plants and need plenty of water.*

RIGHT *This terracotta punnet is planted with gold, grey and green varieties of* Soleirolia soleirolii. *Take care as you put the delicate plants into the compost and try to avoid any pressure on the leaves or you will spoil the effect. I can also see this pot overflowing with variegated strawberry* Fragaria × ananassa '*Variegata*'.

ABOVE *These yellow and white striped pots, containing my favourite box mop-heads, are actually antique, but you could get nearly the same effect with modern machine-made ones. Leave the rim unpainted for detail.*

LEFT *Pyramids of artificial limes look sweet in miniature Tôle tubs. When I was painting these I did use masking tape, as wiggly lines would be inappropriate to the smart look of the tubs.*

RIGHT *On this pot emerald green is given a new slant by being checked with white. I can see the pot as a centrepiece for a summer lunch party in the garden, possibly crammed with chives or bright green parsley.*

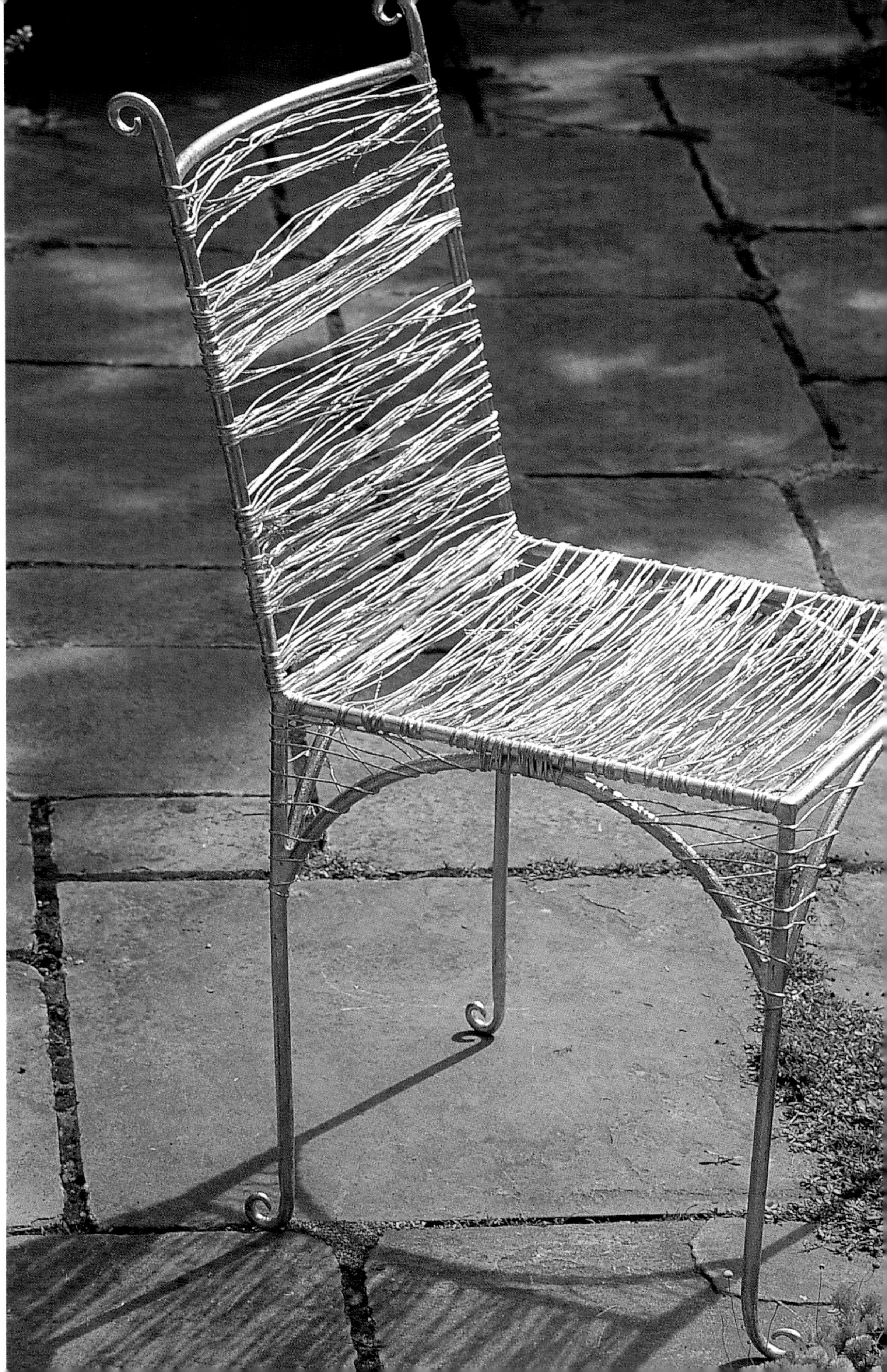

and Decorated

Every garden needs some decoration – it offers you the chance to make your territory unique and reflect your personality. This garden, like most, evolved over a period of time and, when I first saw it, the York stone paving was already *in situ*, together with some curved raised beds.

Curves though, unless they are formal ones, look artificial in small spaces so the first thing I suggested was straightening them up. Meanwhile, a raised platform for a seat was added at the far end of the garden. The owners found a beautiful nineteenth-century cast-iron, fern-patterned bench, which looked rather hard in its white paint. I painted it in an eighteenth-century colour called 'drab' (you need a few dull colours, to make the bright ones sing) that helped to make the back wall recede.

Punctuating the newly squared beds with box balls furnished the garden in winter and created depth by breaking up the long lines into small compartments. Now, with the basic structure sorted out, the fun could begin: the decoration.

The bench acted as a focal point, but it needed setting, and I hit upon the idea of a walk of six Versailles tubs down the main body of the garden. The pairs at either end were painted

LEFT *This cool silvered chair is a favourite. It looks impossibly fragile, and would light up any garden.*

ABOVE *This urn, filled with helichrysum and marguerites which will tolerate some shade, lights a gloomy corner.*
RIGHT *This fine cast-iron bench was originally white, but is now painted in 'drab'.*

with 'powder blue' eggshell, with the middle ones in 'lime white' for variation. Breaking up the colour gave the tubs a casual elegance, and when each was planted with a box mop-head, a satisfying pattern developed, giving the garden new richness and depth.

To enhance the area by the house, I set a box spiral in a large tub striped in matt 'carriage green' and 'lime white' to lead the eye into the garden. Pelargoniums in shiny black pots (like patent leather shoes) and a fake marble pillar, bringing a touch of the theatrical, all play their part.

There is now a deliciously French, almost rococo feel about the garden, which bears its decoration in a light-hearted way. Although the chairs, pots and decorated pillar might sound frivolous, they are what gives this garden its sparkle and glamour.

PLANTING PLAN
6m/20ft wide x 7.5/25ft long

❶ *Magnolia grandiflora*
❷ *Magnolia × loebneri* 'Leonard Messel'
❸ Faux marble pillar topped with ivy-leaved pelargoniums in a black plastic pot
❹ Nineteenth-century bench in 'drab' eggshell
❺ Box balls *(Buxus sempervirens)*
❻ Silver birch tree *(Betula pendula)*
❼ *Rosa glauca*
❽ Miniature Versailles tubs containing pyramids of artificial limes
❾ Versailles tubs planted with box mop-heads surrounded by *Pelargonium* 'Lord Bute'
❿ *Sedum* 'Herbstfreude'
⓫ Modern silver chair
⓬ *Hosta sieboldiana* var. *elegans*
⓭ Box spiral *(Buxus sempervirens)*
⓮ Brighton pier mask (with ivy-leaved *Pelargonium* 'L'Elégante')
⓯ French chairs and tables

Decisive

Planting

No matter how elegant the structure of a garden is, it is the planting that really brings it to life: choice of plant form, colour and habit is crucial to any garden's overall success. Without the evergreen definition and architectural shape created by foliage, it will have no framework. Flower colour adds detail – splashes of black, pink or 'painted' combinations provide instant focus, while white, silver and blue lift a small garden and can be used more extensively than the stronger colours to stunning effect.

I hope that the following very personal selection of favourite planting choices will provide inspiration for your own space.

EVERGREEN STRUCTURE

I look on these plants as the link between house and garden. The trick with them is to make the foreground as visually robust as the background, creating a bridge between the house beyond the garden and the plants within. Evergreens are the living bones – the vital backbone – giving permanence and stability.

No plants give a greater sense of age – that essential quality of timelessness – than box and yew. Winter, spring, summer or autumn, all other plants work well against their solid shapes. Do not listen to people who tell you that yew or box take for ever to grow: once established, yew can put on up to 30cm/12in in a season, while box will grow 15cm/6in during the same time.

Box and yew become more beautiful with each passing year, however, and develop more and more character – a vital quality. Once this framework is in place you will find that all

your other plants look a hundred times more settled. In fact, even brand-new planting will settle quietly into place if you have plenty of established box and yew shapes in your garden to give the new plants that strong background.

These evergreens are the antique furniture of the garden, and their compact roots mean that you can transplant them easily (I would not dream of moving house without my box topiaries). The reason for failure when moving most types of evergreen is that, while most people remember to water the roots, they neglect the leaves – where much of the plant's water is lost. Spray the foliage as well as watering the roots, and you will find that even the largest pieces soon settle into their new home. As for clipping, wait until midsummer, by which time the young leaves will have hardened up and lost that buttery quality.

The bay tree *(Laurus nobilis)* has a noble pedigree, having been cultivated for almost as long as civilization itself. I love to see it grown as larger versions of the box mop-heads, as pyramids in classical terracotta pots framing a door or bench, or even over trellis to make a living porch on a cottage.

As a fantasy, a pavilion, castellated hedge, sentry box or tent fashioned out of yew or box would be out of this world. At a more realistic level, spirals, cones and balls of evergreens all bring instant style to a garden and give it the impression of being well founded. Even if your other planting is not up to scratch, if you can disguise it with a few well-chosen evergreen focal points no one will ever know.

FAR LEFT *This successful combination of seasonal marguerites, helichrysum and tobacco plants would not be nearly so strong without the central pineapple of clipped box to anchor it throughout the year.*
LEFT *A box totem pole is a luxurious thing, for it takes many years to grow and train. This one is probably around twenty years old. If you are patient, of course, you could grow your own.*

SOCIAL CLIMBERS

Climbing plants offer you the chance to turn the most undistinguished architecture into something beautiful. It is their very capacity to be manipulated – trained over an unlovely wall, a stark trellis or a fence – that makes them such a valuable addition to the garden. Plant climbers 35–45cm/12–18in away from the structure that they are to cover; angle them in and water copiously during their first summer – I always put a couple of bricks over their roots to help conserve moisture (particularly with clematis). And if planting near the house, ensure that the roots of magnolias,

BELOW *Beautiful* Clematis florida *'Sieboldii' needs full sun, a sheltered position and, like most clematis, it likes a cool root run. Do not be discouraged when people say it is impossible to grow – with a little care it will surprise you.*

figs, wisteria and so on will not damage its foundations – to be sure consult a qualified surveyor.

If you have a wall that catches the sun, there is no more flattering climber for any house than luxurious, scented wisteria. I love both the lilac and the slightly more unusual white variety, whose scent reminds me of jasmine tea. Wisteria looks marvellous with *Clematis montana* growing through it, but do not let this quick-growing clematis smother the host plant. Or you could combine the soft azure flowers of *Clematis* 'Perle d'Azur' with the large, decorative leaves of the ornamental fruiting vine *Vitis vinifera* 'Purpurea' (whose leaves turn smoky-purple in the autumn) to bring the glamour of the Mediterranean to any terrace, garden or yard.

If you have lime-free soil and a shady wall, try growing camellias. I like *Camellia japonica* 'Lady McCulloch' – an old variety and the best of the stripes, in my opinion. Camellias hate having their flowers warmed up too quickly by the sun after a frosty night, but – being related to the tea plant – appreciate having dregs of tea placed around them as a mulch each morning. I like the singles in softest pink and white best of all: 'Cornish Snow' is a dream, and to see the odd striped camellia in the middle of winter is always a thrill. Finally, *Garrya elliptica*, with its large, soft grey catkins (it is important to ask for the male form), and winter jasmine with primrose-yellow flowers will do well against a shady wall too, as will hellebores, which could happily live at the feet of all these.

Do not forget climbing roses – what they lack in structure they more than make up for in generosity of flower. I particularly like the old varieties; I love the idea that Elizabeth I might have known that grey-leaved rose with soft pink flowers, *Rosa* 'Great Maiden's Blush', just as well as I do. I would not be without the striped *Rosa* 'Variegata di Bologna', which reminds me of loganberries and cream. Many of these climbers are quite content in a shady situation.

ABOVE TOP *The romantic* Wisteria floribunda *'Multijuga', here covering a pergola, needs a sunny position.*
ABOVE *The delicate, smoky colour and architectural leaves of* Vitis vinifera *'Purpurea' are redolent of the Mediterranean.*

HANDSOME FOLIAGE

Any plants with strong architectural character can really alter the look of a place: it is all a matter of personal style. Broadly speaking, weeping plants soften a hard view – the most box-like house, for instance, will be improved by draping it in wisteria or framing it with weeping trees or shrubs, such as silver-leaved weeping pear.

I love to see the elegant profiles of agaves growing tall in urns, breaking up the outline of surrounding buildings or piercing the sky; spiky cordylines and elegant silver astelias perform the same role while tolerating some shade.

Wings of neatly clipped evergreen hedging and low, spreading plants, such as *Cotoneaster horizontalis* and creeping juniper, add a gracious look and help to anchor a house visually to the ground, while the horizontal lines of a low building may be broken up with vertical or fastigiate trees like the Irish yew.

I think magnolia brings architectural quality to any garden. Its beautiful leaves and elegant branch structure make a good foreground subject for looking through to the garden beyond, so try and keep the centre of the tree nice and open.

There is an architectural plant for every situation – it is simply a matter of finding the right one. Strangely enough, many of the most effective architectural shapes are the easiest plants to grow, being perfectly happy in shady conditions under trees. Once you have created the architectural framework for your garden, you can add the details with colour.

FAR RIGHT *In the grey and white* Agave americana *'Mediopicta Alba', architecture and plant life are combined in a striped fantasy.*
RIGHT TOP Melianthus major, *grey architectural foliage at its classiest.*
RIGHT MIDDLE Hosta sieboldiana *var.* elegans. *Aristocratic hostas, best grown in shade, are champagne and caviar to slugs and snails; surround them with grit to protect them.*
RIGHT BELOW Fatsia japonica, *an underrated architectural evergreen.*

BLACK AS LIQUORICE

Beautiful and rare, mysterious and expensive-looking, black flowers are magical. Maybe it is because they are such a good foil to other colours – picture black with lime, pink or white; or with any colour really (except royal blue – the effect is always too cold). Black flowers are not sombre; in fact, they bring excitement to the garden and stop everything else looking bland. Some people say that black tends to make a visual hole in a border. On a large scale, I might agree; when seen from a distance the plants tend to merge into one another. But in a small garden you view the plants close up, so this is not a problem.

I love *Viola* 'Molly Sanderson', chocolate-scented *Cosmos atrosanguineus*, *Fritillaria camschatcensis*, old-fashioned double primroses, irises (especially the bearded *Iris* 'Superstition'), *Geranium phaeum*, *Clematis* 'Royal Velours' and 'Etoile Violette', black aquilegias and *Viola* 'Bowles' Black' self-sown between paving stones.

Black leaves are wonderful, too; they do not have the crudeness that often spoils red or yellow foliage. Dark-leaved *Viola riviniana* 'Purpurea' will grow in the gloomiest spot – even under yew trees. The shiny leaves of the creeping *Ophiopogon planiscapus* 'Nigrescens' are as wicked as liquorice. It is fun to surround a treasure with this useful plant – a spotlight in reverse.

Plants with black flowers and leaves may not be quite so easy to find as the more obvious colours, but they are no more difficult to cultivate.

LEFT *I love the crumpled faces of* Viola *'Eclipse'. Try growing them in terracotta pans or in pots as a row on a windowsill.*
RIGHT TOP Helleborus orientalis, *one of the delights of spring. The blacker the better, if you can find them. They like a shady spot.*
RIGHT BOTTOM Aeonium arboreum *'Atropurpureum'. People always stop and ask me what these extraordinary 'sun-hat' plants are when they see them planted out in pots for the summer.*

WHITE AND BRIGHT

Every garden needs white flowers to bring it to life. They light the garden, enhance other colours and create beautifully subtle reflections. White gives freshness and charm to any scheme.

To indulge in some old-fashioned glamour, create a grey, green and white garden. It would be fun to explore the subtleties of this colour scheme; with no other shades to distract the eye, you need to rely on good lines and different textures and shapes. White Madonna lilies (*Lilium candidum*) or white foxgloves, for instance, towering above grey *Santolina pinnata* subsp. *neapolitana* or *Hosta sieboldiana* var. *elegans* would be good. *Campanula* 'Burghaltii' is a little-known treasure: its white bells suffused with smoky lilac are exquisite and – like alchemilla and the hardy geraniums – if you cut it back hard after flowering, a few weeks later it will begin all over again.

Anemone × *hybrida* 'Honorine Jobert' is a jewel. The flowers on this old variety are the best I know, for not only will she take over from the roses in summer and go on until the first frosts, but she also seems to thrive on neglect and tolerates a considerable amount of shade, from which the pure-white flowers gleam. I like to introduce plenty of grey and silver foliage (page 104) for softness and to spice it up with box or yew topiary.

White tobacco plants mean that you can have scent at the end of the day, and there is nothing quite like white flowers in the cool of the evening. Remember that the elegance of a white garden in summer is all the more enjoyable if you allow yourself a little colour in early spring. After all, no one can live on champagne and smoked salmon all the time!

LEFT *In a mild season, snowdrops nose through in midwinter and by early spring your garden should be covered in enchanting sheets of the honey-scented flowers. You can never have too many of them; both single and double forms are great.*
RIGHT Arisaema candidissimum *has the most dramatic trilobal leaves in soft jade and striped flowers that appear in early summer. I have grown this treasure both in pots and beneath cubes of box, where the spectacular leaves look wonderful.*

A Classic White Border

Apart from box, magnificent hostas and a perennial sweet pea, this narrow border relies on seasonal planting for its impact. It has a white theme: in summer with roses, Madonna lilies, osteospermum daisies and marguerites and in spring with snowdrops. An underplanting of yellow *Narcissus* 'Tête-à-tête' complements the snowdrops perfectly.

I used trellis pyramids, painted the curious grey-turquoise of old French chairs and planted with white roses, to bring height to a border where trees, even if there was room for them, would be too large and gloomy. Their colour contrasts with the plants wonderfully and brings variety to the grey, green and white of the border.

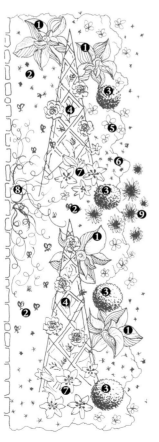

Planting Plan
1.5m/4½ft wide x 6.5m/22ft long

❶ *Hosta sieboldiana* var. *elegans*
❷ *Helichrysum petiolare*
❸ Box balls *(Buxus sempervirens)*
❹ *Rosa* 'Madame Alfred Carrière' on trellis pyramids
❺ White petunias
❻ White Danish marguerites
❼ White lilies
❽ Perennial sweet pea *(Lathyrus latifolius* 'White Pearl')
❾ White-flowered, variegated osteospermum

RIGHT *I always like to make a border develop through the year. This grey, green and white scheme changes subtly each season; white can be dull if you keep it dominant all the time.*

ABOVE *The creamy*
white, perfumed double
flowers of Rosa 'Madame
Alfred Carrière' and the
equally highly scented,
magnificent flowers of
the Madonna lily
(Lilium candidum).

SILVER SURFING

Grey and silver foliage are God's gift to the owners of small gardens, creating the same effect as white walls in a room, enhancing other colours and lending an air of spaciousness. These subtle colours also have a lightness of touch, especially on filigree-like or sculptural foliage; but do not rely on them too heavily. If all the leaves in the garden were silver or grey, it would look anaemic and arid. Two-thirds green to one-third silver is about right to make the silver and grey really glow.

In a temperate climate it is best not to plant any greys until all danger of frost is over. Most silvers and greys (with the exception of hostas and silver-painted ferns) – especially furry-leaved subjects – like hot, dry conditions. Planted with plenty of grit and gravel, they should never need watering once they have established themselves.

Hostas allow you to continue a silver theme into shady areas. The aristocratic *H. sieboldiana* is the best – insist on the variety *elegans*. *Euphorbia characias* subsp. *wulfenii*, whose lime-green flowers against the glaucous leaves create a lovely effect each spring, can do without much sun too. Few roses will tolerate shade, but the grey and plum *Rosa glauca* is an exception and adds useful height.

Helichrysum petiolare is invaluable for underplanting in the summer, when its foaming grey foliage gives a sense of luxury. I put it everywhere, even in the shade. Curiously, in a container combined with other plants, it looks municipal and artificial, but small-leaved helichrysum on its own in a detailed urn looks good by its very understatement.

To take the spotlight in the garden I would choose *Melianthus major* and the statuesque Scotch thistle *(Onopordum acanthium)*. These two plants have made me realize that if a garden is boldly planted, with enough detail as back-up, you do not need to overload it with architectural decoration.

BELOW Convolvulus cneorum *works well in these galvanized buckets, which enable them to enjoy sunlight and are themselves set off by the pink thrift – a classic combination.*

FAR LEFT *Elegant* Artemisia *'Powis Castle' needs full sun and sharp drainage. It sparkles when clipped into a large globe.*

LEFT *The silver-white leaves of* Artemisia ludoviciana, *the texture of felt, always look smart with other silvers and greys.*

TRUE BLUE

Blue is the colour of graciousness and serenity. In gardens it has always represented beauty and luxury, for true-blue flowers – like black ones – are unusual.

In general, although there are warm shades – particularly those with a measure of yellow in their make-up – blue is a cool, receding colour. Like silver, grey and to some extent white, it brings an air of spaciousness to a place. It also conveys a light-hearted feeling to the garden in late summer when everything is looking tired and dusty.

I would love to make a blue garden. My shrubs might include one of the bright blue rosemaries ('Benenden Blue', 'Sissinghurst Blue' or 'Severn Sea') for early spring, 'Mariesii Perfecta' hydrangeas for high summer, maybe planted in large powder-blue Versailles tubs, and a group of *Caryopteris* × *clandonensis* for the autumn. I would add unpainted tubs of

ABOVE *Gentians in the most brilliant blue imaginable. The colour is so intense that if they were larger, they might be vulgar. There is a charming pale blue variety too.*

blue agapanthus, perhaps placed either side of an antique bench – the grandeur of these plants, like orchids, demands simple treatment.

The garden could have brick walls draped with lilac *Wisteria floribunda* 'Multijuga' growing alongside violet clematis. Creamy honeysuckle and white climbing roses would complement them.

Blue pulmonaria, delphiniums, larkspur, anchusa, cornflowers, eryngium (sea holly), herbaceous blue clematis and, somewhere, *Clematis* 'Perle d'Azur' would be underplanted with hundreds of snowdrops (both single and double), to be followed by bright blue *Scilla siberica*. Very pale, or deepest blue, pansies would go well with Pacific Hybrid polyanthus, and I would not despise the humble forget-me-not and the odd clump of bluebells. I should also like to see lemon and cream 'Jack Snipe' daffodils nearby. Blue can look a little cold on its own, and needs lemon, cream, white and perhaps violet and lilac to soften it; masses of grey plants provide visual clarity, and I would weave touches of white everywhere for a bright, contrasting lift.

There is a wonderful claret-blue sweet pea ('Cupani') that I would plant up for the summer, along with electric-blue camassias, vanilla-scented ultramarine petunias and wonderfully scented heliotrope, or cherry pie. And what blue garden would be complete without the ravishing blue Himalayan poppy *(Meconopsis grandis)* in a shady, damp corner?

LEFT *Agapanthus is grand in all its aspects: aristocratic, strappy foliage and great globes of sky-blue flowers. There is a white variety, but it is not as nice. It is inclined to be tender, and looks best grown in ordinary tubs that enhance its nobility – and, if possible, reflected in water.*
ABOVE Meconopsis grandis. *This exquisite blue Himalayan poppy needs a semi-shaded, sheltered position in rich, lime-free soil.*

PAINTED FLOWERS

If any kind of flower is theatrical, a painted one is. By 'painted' I mean, of course, one with strong markings in contrasting colours. There is something charmingly artificial about them. Like black flowers, they need to be planted in small numbers to give the garden a lift here and there. An entire border of black flowers would look lifeless; one containing nothing but black and white pansies mixed with striped petunias would be distracting, to say the least. But touches of both, here and there – what could be nicer?

Use painted flowers sparingly, somewhere prominent and in the light (the plainer the background, the better). They look best planted generously, with nothing else, in a container: striped *Tulipa* 'Estella Rijnveld' in one big pot, for instance, would be stunning.

As for permanently planted subjects, a white tree peony with raspberry-coloured blotches would look fabulous against a hedge. A strip of raspberry-ripple *Rosa gallica* 'Versicolor' (also called Rosa Mundi) bordering a path would look just right; and regularly placed maroon and white old-fashioned pinks, such as *Dianthus* 'Dad's' (or 'Gran's') Favourite', would stop a silver and white border becoming boring.

I have many other favourite painted flowers, among them striped petunias; striped tulips; *Rosa* 'Variegata di Bologna' and picoteed 'Baron Girod de l'Ain';

BELOW Pelargonium *'Splendide' is the most wonderful plant, with matt grey leaves. It needs full sun and should be planted on its own in pots in a place where it will naturally take the spotlight.*

ABOVE Rosa gallica *'Versicolor'* is an old rose that dates at least from the sixteenth century. It is good grown as low hedges and, although it flowers only once in a summer, when it is out the clusters of raspberry-ripple petals are, as you can see, sensational.

painted poppies; *Hosta sieboldiana* 'Frances Williams'; the Japanese fern *Athyrium niponicum* var. *pictum*; *Cistus ladanifer*, which has white flowers blotched with purple; 1.5m/5ft-high *Paeonia rockii*; *Silybum marianum*; *Jasminum officinale* 'Argenteo-variegatum' with its variegated and pink-tipped leaves; ornamental cabbages; and auriculas, with their King-Charles-spaniel faces.

Painted flowers are star performers, but – like prima donnas – they are best appreciated in small doses.

STRONG PINKS

From softest rose through shocking-pink to deepest raspberry, pink is high fashion. Do not be afraid of pink – it warms up a garden on the drabbest day and, even at its brightest, is never strident (unlike strong reds, which can be difficult to use in a small garden, except in moderation).

At its most delicate, nothing is more feminine, but pink has so many moods – at its strongest, it can be raffish, sensuous and audacious. Shocking-pink and white petunias remind me of bright summer awnings; they tumble beautifully and are sensational in a container mixed with *Pelargonium* 'Lord Bute'.

Apricot-pink can look lovely, especially when seen in the coppery-pink flowers of *Rosa* 'Albertine', but I would keep it away from the other shades of pink, instead combining apricot with cream, light blue, lemon or grey. However, the hundreds of perfect little clear-pink roses produced by the climbing rose 'New Dawn' would go with any other type of pink; or, you could grow it together with the smoky blue clematis 'Perle d'Azur', the effect is enchanting. All three climbers will tolerate a north wall.

Three other plants show how rich the many shades of pink can be. Nothing is grander than the sugar-pink, sweetly scented *Crinum × powellii* against a warm wall in early autumn. Sealing-wax-pink nerines (*Nerine bowdenii*) are spectacular, even later in the year. And if you can, try and obtain the expensive-looking pink *Clematis* 'Etoile Rose', for it is truly wonderful.

As for the old-fashioned roses, admittedly they do not have a long flowering season (although quite a few are recurrent) and their structure is not especially interesting, but when those pink blooms are out – wow! What is more, they are easy to grow, their flower colour goes with almost everything, especially green (perhaps because their pink has a dash of blue in it) and they seem to give a garden a sense of history.

RIGHT Clematis *'Madame Julia Correvon'. This exquisite creature is not difficult to grow and the indescribable pink of her flowers, quite apart from their formation, is one of the miracles of summer.*
LEFT TOP *Quartered* Rosa *'Charles de Mills'. No garden feels complete without old-fashioned roses such as this. Like box, yew and wisteria, they give a place a sense of history.*
LEFT BOTTOM Clematis *'Rouge Cardinal'. Like all clematis, this would be happy growing through other plants. It would look lovely growing through soft pink roses, perhaps with the deeper purple bells of* Cobaea scandens *near by.*

VENETIAN RED

Somewhere between black and pink lies another shade, which I would hesitate to call purple (since this can look crude if the shade is wrong), yet is darker than crimson. The best way I can describe it is by comparing it to the deep red of a rich claret. Like black flowers, deep red ones should be seen as an indulgence and used to highlight areas of the garden and inject a drop of pure luxury.

Variations of deep red occur in some of the old roses, such as the ancient but tough Gallica rose varieties – 'Charles de Mills' and 'Tuscany Superb' to name but two. These are perfect for small gardens: tolerant of some shade, extremely long-lived and do not grow too large (1.2-1.5m/ 4-5ft). They require little pruning and, although they flower only once in the early summer, it is with such generosity and heavenly scent that one could forgive them almost anything. Two other roses with rich, dark flowers whose delights I want to pass on are 'Guinée' (a near-black climber that is perfect for a sunny wall) and the rather rare 'Louis XIV' (which grows to no more than 45cm/18in high and could even be grown in a pot on a windowsill).

Tulips come in some marvellous deep reds: I can never decide whether I prefer 'Queen of Night' for its slightly superior colour or 'Black Parrot' (which is not really black, but a deep claret), with its quirky, seventeenth-century appearance. Plant tulips deep – about three times the height of the bulb is a good rule of thumb – in mid to late autumn, but try not to grow them in the same place two years running or you risk their contracting the disease known as 'tulip fire'. Tulips always look great in large tubs or ornamental pots. Growing them in pots also gives them some protection from slugs and snails – and you can further deter these attackers by smearing a ring of Vaseline around the rim of the pot.

Clematis viticella 'Purpurea Plena Elegans' reminds me of Parma violets. Ruby/slate-coloured *Helleborus orientalis* 'Vulcan' will happily tolerate shade and bring a touch of glamour to winter, while I can think of nothing nicer than a bed of the deepest red, scented wallflowers basking in the sun on the first day of spring.

RIGHT *Chocolate-scented* Cosmos atrosanguineus. *Fully grown plants are offered by the better garden centres around mid-summer. I like to grow them singly in pots, and place one or two near a seat or step in the sun where they always provoke comment.*
FAR RIGHT *Sumptuous 'Queen of Night' tulips look really smart in May. For extra style, grow this or 'Black Parrot' with white Lily-flowered tulips in alternate containers.*
BELOW RIGHT Rosa *'Nuits de Young' is one of the Moss roses popular in the nineteenth century. In my opinion, it is time for a revival of antique roses; they really bring atmosphere and even one or two will bring old-fashioned glamour to the smallest space.*

A PINK BORDER

The theme for this border sprang from the owner's favourite colour – it was as simple as that. We found a most beautiful petunia, deep raspberry and elegantly veined in black – the effect was of raw silk – and took it from there. Each year we work out different combinations of pink, white and silver: sometimes we try marguerites with pink and white striped petunias and plenty of small silver-leaved helichrysum; another year we included a little pale blue lobelia.

To date, I think the country-looking cosmos have been the most successful. With deadheading and a little gentle misting on hot summer nights, these plants are very easy to look after. The informal flowers contrast nicely with the box topiary.

LEFT *Deep pink, shell-pink and white cosmos bring a breath of the country to this inner-city garden. Their simple shapes work well in the luxurious topiary setting.*

PLANTING PLAN   6m/20ft wide × 2m/5½ft long

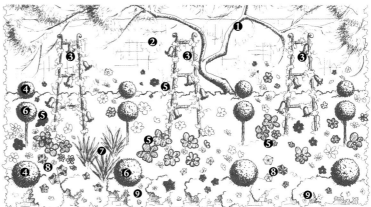

❶ Silver-leaved willow
❷ *Wisteria sinensis* on dark green trellis walls
❸ White *Cobaea scandens* on metal rose supports
❹ Box balls *(Buxus sempervirens)*
❺ Mixed *Cosmos bipinnatus* 'Sonata'
❻ Box mop-heads *(Buxus sempervirens)*
❼ *Iris pallida* 'Variegata'
❽ Pink and white striped petunias
❾ *Convolvulus althaeoides*

Getting
it together

Although it is still fairly young, as somebody recently remarked, my new garden in Thompson Road seems to be a distillation of all my design ideas. Rather to my surprise, however, I find that my taste is becoming simpler and more classical – I am proud of my past designs, but I am not sure if I would put so much in them now.

As the plants establish themselves, it is hard to believe that the garden is the same rough old place I took on a short time ago; it is now beginning to take shape. I would not have missed a minute of all the work that went into it. Here, as well as the inspiration for its present form, the garden at Villandry, I would like to show you my small garden in its different stages. I hope you like it.

MY GARDEN'S INSPIRATIONS

BELOW AND RIGHT *The earthy tang of ornamental cabbages, as well as the aroma of smouldering logs in the distance, always remind me of Villandry (below) in the autumn. Back home, the season is not complete without them. The cabbages are so decorative in their creams, sea greens, pinks and magentas that they seem to warm the garden like voluptuous cabbage roses. I like to plant them close, like chocolates in a box. At Villandry, any suggestion of monotony is broken by the standard roses; my equivalents are box mop-heads.*

The potager at Villandry – the famous château garden on the banks of the River Loire – was the inspiration behind my new garden. It probably sounds extraordinary that such a large place could inspire such a small one, but ever since I have been an adult, I cannot help seeing everything as a stage set. Theatre is in my blood, and it is hard to break the habit! Villandry is grandeur and simplicity – a combination I have always loved – rolled into one.

From the darkest green paint of my window frames and doors to stained green trellis walls topped with decorative finials, you can see the influence of Villandry – even if there is a rather remarkable difference in size. There is the topiary (at which French gardeners excel); my interpretation is mop-heads of box and bay in swag pots. I try to bring a breath of rural France to my garden with a large trellis pyramid painted in the soft, worn-out blue that I associate with old French chairs.

I have learned through experience that large Versailles tubs, another idea borrowed from Villandry, are too dominating for my small space. Nevertheless, inspired by eighteenth-century Sèvres porcelain miniatures, I bought tiny versions in wood and planted them with box mop-heads to the same scale. I enjoy them at my window as I write.

There are large stone urns near the entrance to Villandry and I have some at Thompson Road; mine are in the garden and not outside my front door, I hasten to add! I usually recommend wall fountains for town gardens but my fountains are the single slim jets found in France. A combination of slightly overgrown brick and flagstones for the floor surfaces suggests the antiquity and rustic charm of the large French garden. I do not think my Fowler Pink house walls (the more worn-looking they become, the more I will like them) are a bad substitute for castle walls of old limestone.

MY GARDEN'S INCARNATIONS

It was important to me to make the outlines of my garden plain, for I had a little plan. I wanted to try out some ideas within the overall structure just for fun.

This stage began with my favourite 2m/6½ft urns. The original idea was to decorate one with a malachite effect, another in distressed gold and the third, nearest the house, with pink marbling. Then I painted the shed – inherited from the previous owner – in blue and white stripes. It provided a central focus on the far wall and its stripes were echoed in grey and black on a pair of large Versailles tubs containing standards of *Fuchsia* 'Checkerboard'.

I pierced the gravel floor beneath the tubs with box balls, while a pair of nineteenth-century, French conservatory chairs, painted blue and white, and an emerald-coloured table provided the finishing touches.

However, even before I had completed the marbling on the pink urn, I decided that the party was over. Too much colour and too many features simply looked too busy. But at least the original wreck had been cleared, and the hard landscaping was now firmly in place.

In the new plan, a more classical mood, more closely inspired by the grandeur and simplicity of the Villandry potager, prevails. The gravel provided a base for the flagstones and second-hand bricks; I planted soleirolia and wall daisies to soften the paving. With the bleak surroundings of the garden, everything within it needed to be based on strong foundations – but to be as soft-looking and as verdant as possible.

The different stages of my new garden (far left, top to bottom), from wasteland, through experimental paint effects to the present (left). I enjoyed the bright paint effects while they lasted but never really took them too seriously. On reflection, these early stages show how not to do grandeur and simplicity!

PLANTING MY GARDEN

This aspect of the garden I have enjoyed more than anything else. With the back of the house in shade for most of the day, the garden has little sun – indeed, the sun never reaches it in the winter, which is unfortunate, as I have a penchant for Mediterranean plants – and this has influenced my choice.

I grow the rare grey and white striped *Agave americana* 'Mediopicta Alba' in the tall urns because they love the sharp drainage I can give them in the stone containers. The height of the urns also means that they catch any available sunshine.

The *Paeonia rockii*, which came to me from the south of France, is flourishing. She has just given me two white silk flowers blotched with raspberry, the size of dinner-plates. I was certain I had lost her in the move from my previous garden, but she survived the indignity of living in a plastic bag for over a year while the new garden was being constructed. Other favourites are the banana-scented vigorous white *Rosa mulliganii*, thriving in a shady corner, and *R.* 'Baron Girod de l'Ain' with its lovely red velvet flowers, edged in creamy white.

I cannot decide whether to surround the swag-pots with white tobacco flowers this summer, or try old-fashioned white geraniums. I might have 'Lord Bute' pelargoniums with pale blue daisies in the sink; white marguerites, lilies and daturas might be nice. Perhaps I will make the whole scheme white. A garden is never finished; one is endlessly experimenting – what fun it all is. And there is always next summer.

FAR RIGHT *Box mop-heads give permanent structure to this planting. With them in place, you can change the plants beneath on a whim. I like to see masses of one variety in a container; that way you really appreciate the beauty of one flower – here dusty pink tulips – properly.*
ABOVE RIGHT *Narcissus 'Tête-à-tête' planted* en masse *look generous with the dark green of the wooden container.*
RIGHT *I brought this stone sink from my previous garden. Again, a mass of flowers, in this case pansies, really makes an impact.*

4.5m/16ft wide × 11m/36ft long

❶ *Agave americana* 'Mediopicta Alba'

❷ Bay mop-heads *(Laurus nobilis)* in terracotta swag-pots

❸ *Hedera canariensis* 'Gloire de Marengo'

❹ *Rosa* 'Variegata di Bologna' on pyramid

❺ *Clematis* 'Etoile Rose'

❻ *Wisteria sinensis* 'Alba'

❼ *Rosa* 'Baron Girod de l'Ain'

❽ *Astelia chathamica*

❾ *Melianthus major*

❿ Bearded *Iris* 'Superstition'

⓫ Yew hedge *(Taxus baccata)*

⓬ Old stone sink with black and white pansies

⓭ *Paeonia rockii*

⓮ Box mop-heads and balls *(Buxus sempervirens)*

⓯ *Rosa* 'Rosa 'Honorine de Brabant'

⓰ *Rosa × odorata* 'Viridiflora'

⓱ *Hosta sieboldiana* var. 'Elegans'

⓲ Black *Helleborus orientals*

⓳ *Rosa* 'Madame Alfred Carrière'

⓴ *Clematis* 'Etoile Violette'

㉑ *Rosa* 'Mermaid'

125

LEFT *The old York flagstones are now looking more settled. After only a year, and a wet winter and spring, my plans are daily becoming more and more of a reality.*

Maintenance

When I lived in a small flat, I found that unless I was scrupulously tidy, in no time at all the place resembled a tip. This is equally true of small gardens. In little spaces, especially in towns, absolutely everything is under the spotlight; in large places you can get away with a lot more. In a small garden just sweeping makes a difference you can see immediately. Here, very briefly, are what I regard as the essentials of maintaining small gardens.

Buying Tools

I always buy the best tools I can; they are cheaper in the long run and are a pleasure to use. That sounds like an advertisement, but it is true. The basics you will need are:

- secateurs
- a sharpening stone
- a trowel and a border fork
- a hoe (buy stainless-steel as it goes through the soil more easily)
- stout gloves
- a kneeling mat

A good-quality watering can is also a necessity. And if you can arrange to have an outside tap installed – to which you can attach a hose – you will never regret it.

Watering and Feeding

I dislike permanent visible watering systems; all those tubes look ugly and in any case most people find using a watering can or a hose and giving their plants a drink on a warm summer night quite soothing.

It is no good wetting just the top of the soil as this encourages the feeding roots to reach up to the surface; what most things need is a long, deep drink. In a temperate climate, lawns need nothing more than a good soaking twice a week when the weather is hot; start at the first sign of any hot weather. Soil is dry near walls, so keep a special eye on young climbers until they get established.

Try to water either first thing in the morning or late in the afternoon. Avoid watering anything in full sun, if possible, as water will quickly evaporate from the surface. If something is collapsing before your eyes and you really have to water it, keep any droplets off the leaves and flowers so as to avoid ugly scorch marks. Spraying leaves with water from a hose is a good way to dislodge pests.

Feed plants – for most purposes a general all-purpose fertilizer will do, applied in the spring and at intervals through the growing season – but never when the soil is dry. Always follow the manufacturer's instructions to the letter! To my shame, I once killed an entire border by misplaced – or ignorant – generosity. Do not be put off by my mistakes, though: a foliar feed, especially, is a wonderful tonic in summer, particularly for a plant that seems to be failing.

For topiary, feed box and bay with seaweed liquid-feed occasionally; feed yew with dried blood.

Placing and Planting

Some plants have special soil requirements. For instance, camellias and most gentians are lime-haters. Most plant books will give you the correct information but there are a couple of tips that other books often neglect to mention. First, make friends with the people in your local garden centre and do not be afraid to ask for their advice about what is suitable to plant in your area; second, take a stroll around your neighbourhood to see which plants do well for other people. If you want something that is not suited to your soil, you need to plant it in a special compost – grow camellias, for instance, in ericaceous compost.

The most common fault when planting is to overcrowd. I have done it myself. Luxury is great – plants grouped together usually look better than when placed singly or too widely apart – but crowding is not; the plants will be unhappy.

Pruning and Training

The most important thing about pruning is not to be afraid of it. Generally speaking it will always do a plant more good than harm. Here are a few tips I have picked up over the years relating to the plants I use a lot.

First remove any dead wood, then cut away any inward-growing, or crossing, branches as they will chafe. Remember when training shrubs, trees and roses you want to aim for a shape that roughly resembles an outstretched hand – in other words, open in the centre with equal spaces separating each branch.

A very general pruning rule is that plants that flower before mid-summer are best pruned after flowering and those that flower later are best left until following spring. However there are exceptions – such as some roses and clematis – so you will need to check the requirements of each plant. The latest thinking favours letting the wound heal naturally in the air, rather than sealing it. Whatever you are pruning, try to cut the stem at an angle so that rainwater will run off it.

Dead-heading encourages the plant to continue flowering by preventing it from making seedheads. Once seed has been made, the chief function of the flower – attracting pollinating insects – is done. Dead-heading also saves the plant the huge effort of making seed. Blunt-ended florist's scissors are excellent for this task. As you do it, cut back the whole flower, including the seed-chamber, to the nearest new bud or leaf juncture.

Climbers need to be trained on wires stretched horizontally between vine-eyes (about 13cm/5in long) spaced 60-90cm/2-3ft apart. These lines should be spaced 15-18in apart. I use twists of specially made dark green plastic to attach the plant to the wire gently.

People get confused about wisteria. With a young plant you want to aim for about five main stems that spread out horizontally. These main stems (leaders) will develop leafy tendrils as the summer goes on. When your plant has filled the space you want it to, cut these tendrils back to the sixth bud in early summer (taking care not to cut the spurs on which the flowers form). In the late winter of the following year, cut these same sprigs back to two buds. Repeat the process each year and, providing you have given your wisteria a place in the sun, you will be rewarded with great racemes of scented flowers. What could be simpler?

I have a weakness for agaves but, like most plants, they can develop the odd damaged leaf. If so, in the summer, when the weather is warm, cut these cleanly away from the plant with a bread knife or pruning knife. Do not water for a couple of days and in a short space of time the plant will produce new, healthy leaves.

Bay trees should be trimmed with secateurs, not shears, so that the remaining leaves can be kept intact. They look hideous if the large leaves are, if you will excuse the expression, half-cut. Box and yew can be pruned with shears. Be brave when you shape, but remember that it is better to cut too little and then cut more than spoil a shape by cutting too much. Keep standing back to assess your work from different angles.

Caring for Containers

The rules of pot gardening are different from those for growing plants in the ground. The plants themselves are much more vulnerable to the vagaries of the climate, relying almost totally on their owners for food and drink.

Because a potted plant's catchment area is so small – compared to that of something living in the earth – the soil in a container can still be dry even after it has rained heavily. As with all watering, do the job more thoroughly than you might at first suppose necessary and, if the soil was dry in the first place, water initially and then return. When the water bubbles out from the base of the pot, you know that the job has been done properly. Water containers every day when the weather is hot and feed every other week in the summer months.

I like to plant box in half general purpose compost and half John Innes No 3. Box likes to be kept moist, but do not keep it saturated.

I never bother to change the compost in large containers but, if something appears to be suffering as a result of becoming pot-bound, I might scrape away the surface and replace the top layer with fresh compost. A plant will often flower better when it is pot-bound. You can also shock plants in containers into flowering by depriving them of water. I have used this treatment successfully with camellias.

To prepare a Versailles tub, remove some of the base slats to allow for drainage. Then use a heavy-duty plastic bag (I use trimmed builder's or compost bags) and drawing pins to line the base and sides of the tub, protecting the wood. Use pieces of broken terracotta pots to improve drainage and stop the compost leaching through the drainage holes.

Wooden barrels need five or six holes drilled in their bases to allow drainage – you could ask the retailer to do this for you. Make the holes about 1.5cm/½in in diameter. Galvanized florists' buckets need these holes too, but make them slightly smaller.

A Planting Programme for a Container

One of my favourite container plantings is a central mop-head of box for permanent structure with seasonal planting around the edges. Briefly, my programme for achieving this is as follows:

Early Winter

I plant tulips deeply (at about three times the depth of the bulb). If tulips are not for you, fill the pots with tiny pink and white cyclamen or winter pansies (my favourites are the deep blue or white ones with black centres).

Late Spring

Once the tulips (or whatever) have flowered, and any danger of frosts has passed, I dig them up and plant my summer flowers. I am particularly fond of white and silver themes using lime-green tobacco flower, white marguerites (try to find the Danish, grey-leaved variety) and the small-leaved, grey helichrysum.

Mid autumn

Remove the lot and dress up the pots with sea-green, pink and purple ornamental cabbages.

Pests and other problems

The best thing to do with leaves infested with fungus is to remove them as quickly as possible.

Grit around the base of hostas will discourage slugs and snails, but growing them in a pot with a ring of Vaseline around the brim is foolproof. By all means go around with a torch at night to catch these creatures at work if you like, but I find it easier to discourage them by removing one of their main food sources: dead and diseased leaves.

Try not to let real thugs like dandelions, ground elder (or bishop's weed), bindweed, docks, nettles and thistles get established in the first place. Be vigilant and pull up seedlings when you see them –

you will soon get to know their leaves. Chickweed, wild cress and other annual wildlings are less worrying as they are easy to get rid of, but try not to let any of these characters – especially dandelions – make seedheads, as this is how they spread. In the case of the thugs, when you pull them out, make sure you get the whole root. Otherwise the plant will shoot again from underground.

An old kitchen knife is useful for extracting weeds from between paving stones and other difficult places to reach. And you will be amazed at how much easier things are to pull out when the ground is wet.

I dislike using pesticides, fungicides and chemical weed-killers; keeping a vigilant eye on what is happening in your plot (much more feasible in a small space than a large one) is a better way to garden. If you make sure you take good care of them you should be able to keep away from these potions unless it is absolutely necessary.

When I do resort to pesticides and fungicides, I spray with systemic ones (which are absorbed into the plant itself, and protect against further attacks). Wear a mask and eye protection and do not spray on a windy day. Keep the spray away from food stuffs, pets and children and scrupulously follow the manufacturer's instructions.

Finally, if you grow mop-heads, as I do, and local cats develop a penchant for giving themselves a manicure on the little trunks, discourage them with a wigwam of florist's sticks around the base. If they foul on your patch, bury or clear up their mess straight away and put down some repellent.

Inspirations and Sources

GARDEN CENTRES AND
PLANT STOCKISTS

**Jacques Amand International
Bulbs**
The Nurseries
Clamp Hill
Stanmore
Middlesex HA7 3JS
Tel 0208 420 7110
*Well-known bulb specialists.
Their stock includes 'Black Parrot'
tulips.*

David Austin Roses
Bowling Green Lane
Albrighton
Wolverhampton WV7 3HB
Tel 0190 2376 300
*'English' roses – new varieties
with the charm of the 'old
fashioneds'.*

Avant Garden
77 Ledbury Road
London W11 2AG
Tel 0181 747 1794
*Wire topiary frames, obelisks and
hand-made planters in lead and
terracotta.*

Peter Beales Roses
London Road
Attleborough
Norfolk NR17 1AY
Tel 01953 454707
Large selection of roses.

Caddicks Clematis
Lymm Road
Thelwall
Warrington
Cheshire
Tel 01925 757196
*Excellent clematis nursery – they
stock the superb 'Etoile Rose'.*

The Beth Chatto Gardens
Elmstead Market
Colchester
CO7 7DB
Tel 01206 822007
The place to go for rare plants.

Clifton Nurseries
5a Clifton Villas
London W9 2PH
Tel 0171 289 6851
*Stocks containers, architectural
items, topiary and unusual plants;
also original and reproduction
chairs and wall-fountains.*

The Conran Shop Ltd
Michelin House
81 Fulham Road
London SW3 6RD
Tel 0171 589 7401
*Plants, modern garden furniture
and accessories.*

Andrew Crace
Bourne Lane
Much Hadham
Hertfordshire SG10 6ER
Tel 01279 842685
*Classic wooden garden furniture
and accessories.*

Fibrex Nurseries
Honeybourne Road
Pebworth
Stratford-on-Avon
Warwickshire CV37 8XP
Tel 01789 720788
*Rare pelargoniums including
'Lord Bute' and 'Splendide'.
Large collection of decorative ivies
and rare hellebores.*

The General Trading Company Ltd
144 Sloane Street
London SW1X 9BL
Tel 0171 730 0411
Unusual garden furniture and accessories.

Langley Boxwood Nursery
Rake
Near Liss
Hampshire GU33 7JL
Tel 01730 894467
Holds the National Collection of box (Buxus). *Huge choice of box and yew topiary, hedging etc.*

Marston & Langinger
192 Ebury Street
London SW1W 8UP
Tel 0171 824 8818
Although this firm are best known for their conservatories, they have a range of wrought-iron garden furniture and accessories too.

Peter Jones
Sloane Square
London SW1W 8EL
Tel 0171 730 3434
Garden tools, garden furniture and outdoor living departments. John Lewis has branches all over the country.

Rassells Nursery
78–80 Earls Court Road
London W8 6EQ
Tel 0171 937 0481
Unusual terracotta and rare plants.

Roualeyn Fucshias
Roualeyn Nursery
Trefriw
Conway
North Wales LL27 0SX
Tel 01492 640548
Fucshias including 'Checkerboard'. Older types such as this are, if anything, easier to grow than the more modern ones.

LANTERNS

Colefax & Fowler
39 Brook Street
London W1
Tel 0171 493 2231
Classical, French-style reproduction wall lanterns.

Charles Edwards
582 King's Road
London SW6 2DY
Tel 0171 736 8490
More flamboyant lanterns than those at Colefax & Fowler. Both firms are excellent – it just depends on what is suitable for the situation..

PAINT SHOPS AND MANUFACTURERS

Farrow & Ball
249 Fulham Road
London SW3 6HY
Tel 0171 351 0273
'Fowler Pink' from Farrow and Ball's National Trust range. 'Powder Blue' and 'Lime White' are other favourites.

Papers & Paints
4 Park Walk
London SW10 0AD
Tel 0171 352 8626.
First-class paint shop. The owner is an expert on historic paints.

URNS, SWAG-POTS AND GARDEN CONSTRUCTION

Adela Construction and Landscapes
Frensham Garden Centre
Farnham
Surrey GU10 3BP
Tel 01252 794555
Constructed my garden.

Haddonstone Ltd
The Forge House
East Haddon
Northampton NN6 8DB
Tel 01604 770711
Stone urns and balls etc.

Oak Joinery
49a Beacon Road
Lewisham
London SE13 6ED
Tel 0181 297 2993
*Bespoke wood turners and
architectural joiners.*

Patio Pottery
155 Battersea Park Road
London SW8 4BU
Tel 0171 622 9525
*Italian swag-pots and French-style
cast-iron urns.*

Spanish Pots
265 Mitcham Lane
London SW16 6BQ
Tel 0181 664 6602
*An excellent selection of hand-
made Spanish pots, old and new.*

**David Williams Carpentry and
Joinery**
42 Wellington Road
Sandhurst
Berkshire GU47 9AY
Tel 01344 773572
Carpentry and joinery of all types.

WATER FIXTURES

Anthony Archer-Wills
New Barn Nursery
Broadford Bridge Road
West Chiltington
West Sussex RH20 2LF
Tel 01798 813204
*Water specialist and consultant
designer.*

Ian Spicer – Inland Waterscapes
New Barn Nursery
Broadford Bridge Road
West Chiltington
West Sussex RH20 2LF
Tel 01798 812007
*These firms are based at the same
address and they often work
together. This a construction
company specializing in water.*

GARDEN VISITING

The National Gardens Scheme
Tel 01483 211535
*There is no annual membership.
You buy the Gardens of England
and Wales Open for Charity
guide from a bookshop or
newsagent and then pay a modest
entrance fee at each garden.*

The National Trust
Tel 0181 315 1111
and
The National Trust for Scotland
Tel 0131 226 5922
*Many of The National Trust's
larger properties have plant
stalls – often with unusual plants
for sale.*

The Royal Horticultural Society
Tel 01483 224 234
Wisley
Surrey
(also regional branches)
*First-class garden centre with a
huge gardening bookshop.*

Index

Page numbers in *italic* refer to illustration captions and planting schemes.

planting schemes *49*, *65*, *88*, 91-115
  black schemes 99
  blue schemes 106-7
  climbing plants 58, 94-5
  evergreen plants 92-3
  foliage 96
  grey and silver foliage 104
  'painted' flowers 108-9
  pink schemes 110, 115
  red schemes 112
  white schemes 101-2
  see also border schemes
polyanthus 107
pools 32-41
  formal pools 31, *32*, 35, *35*, 41, *41*, 64
  informal pools 36, *36*, 41
  lighting 31, 41, 47, *49*
  marginal plants 36
  see also fountains
poppies 107, *107*, 108
positioning plants 127
primroses 99
Primula 56, 73
  denticulata 36
pruning 127
pulmonaria 107
pumps *36*

R

Ranunculus 82
red planting schemes 112
Rheum palmatum
  'Atrosanguineum' 36, *36*
rock rose 56, *57*
  see also Helianthemum
roof gardens 20, 27-9, *27*, *29*
Rosa 9, 36, 110
  'Albertine' 110
  'Baron Girod de l'Ain' 108, 122
  'Charles de Mills' *110*, 112
  Gallica roses 112
  gallica 'Versicolor' 108, *109*
  glauca 88, 104
  'Great Maiden's Blush' 95

'Guinée' 58, 112
'Leverkusen' 58
'Louis XIV' 112
'Madame Alfred Carrière' 58, 73, *102*, *103*
'Mermaid' 19, 58
mulliganii 122
'New Dawn' 110
'Nuits de Young' *112*
'Tuscany Superb' 112
'Variegata di Bologna' 95, 108
'Zigeunerknabe' 64, *65*
Rosmarinus (rosemary) 56
  'Benenden Blue' 106
  'Severn Sea' 106
  'Sissinghurst Blue' 106

S

Sackville-West, Vita 9
Santolina pinnata subsp. *neapolitana* 101
saxifrage 56
scale 15, 16, 27-9, 32
Scilla siberica 107
Scotch thistle 104
screening 18, 19
sea holly 107
secluded gardens 18, 19, 48
Sedum 'Herbstfreude' *88*
Sempervivum tectorum (house leeks) *57*, 58
shade, planting in *88*, 95, 96, 101, 104, 112, 122
silver birch *88*
Silybum marianum 109
Sissinghurst Castle 9, 51
slugs and snails 129
snowdrops 56, *101*, 102, 107
Soleirolia soleirolii 24, 54, 63, *63*, 64, *65*, 85, 121
space
  enlarging 15, 18-19, 24
  illusions of 15, 23, *23*
staircases *49, 85*
statues and figures 71, *71, 74*
  lighting 48, *49*
steps *24*

stone balls *24*, 71
stone furniture 53, 64, *65*
stone paving 54, *54*, 118
stone sinks 10, *36*, 38, *122*
swag-pots 80, *81*, 118
sweet peas *102*, 107
Symplocarpus foetidus 36

T

terracotta pots 61, *61*, 73, *73*, 85
thrift 56
Thymus serpyllum 56
tobacco flowers 73, *93*, 101, 122, 129
Tôle tubs 85
tools 126
topiary 16, 53, 93, 118
  see also Buxus sempervirens
Trachycarpus fortunei 29, *29*
tree peonies 108
trellis 10, 15, 20-1, *20*, 58, 71, *71*
  diamond and diagonally squared trellis 20-1
  proportions 21
  squared trellis 20, 21, *49*
  staining 21
trellis pyramids 102, 118
trompe l'oeil 15, 23, *23*
Tulipa 81, 122, 128
  'Black Parrot' 112
  'Estella Rijnveld' 108
  planting 112
  in pots 112
  'Queen of Night' 112, *112*

U

urns 13, 16, 80, *81, 88*, 118, 121
  lighting 42, 47, *47*
  painted 71

V

Versailles 20, 21
Versailles tubs 47, *73*, 80, *82*, 87-8, *88*, 118, 121, 128
Villandry 118, *118*, 121

Viola
  'Bowles' Black' 99
  'Eclipse' 99
  'Molly Sanderson' *82*, 99
  riviniana 'Purpurea' 99
vistas 16, 18-19
Vitis vinifera 'Purpurea' 95, *95*

W

wall daisies 56, 58, 121
wall features 71, *71*
  see also masks
wall-fountains 32, *35*, 38, 48
  see also lion's mask fountains
wallflowers 112
walls
  climbing plants 58
  painted 68, *68*, 71, *71*, 118
  white walls 68
water features *see* fountains; pools
water iris 36
watering 126
  containers 129
watering-cans 10, 51, 74
weeds 129
white flowers 101-2
White Garden, Hidcote *10*
White Garden, Sissinghurst 9, *9*
willow 16, *115*
window boxes 73
windowsills 72-3
winter jasmine 95
Wisteria 19, 71, 95, 96
  floribunda 'Multijuga' 95, 107
  sinensis 115
  pruning 127
woodland effects 19, *19*

Y

yew 53, 92, 93, 96, 126, 128
York stone 54

Acknowledgments

I would like to thank the following people for making this book special. Tom Windross who has worked so hard, selflessly and effectively for my voice to be heard. Jo Grey for her beautiful artwork and Susan Berry for her elegant construction.

Jo Christian, Caroline Hillier, Kate Cave, Anne Fraser and Frances Lincoln have all been wonderfully supportive – Frances, especially, for believing in me at the outset. The same is true of that master of light Andrew Lawson and Judy Dod, his charming assistant.

Ann Collett, Erica Hunningher and Yvonne Adams have always been there for me with kindness, wisdom and encouragement. I am also grateful to Ronnie D'Silva, Richard Coates and Neil Phelps. Paul Hollis, too, for his perception and determination on my behalf.

Jill and Tom White, my delightful neighbours and friends who have suddenly appeared with a plate of smoked salmon or my favourite shepherd's pie. And last, but not least, my mother and father, Pam Deacon and Clem Noel, for showing me so many beautiful and inspirational places.

Publisher's Acknowledgements
Project Editor Sue Berry
Art Editor Jo Grey
Editor Tom Windross
Picture Research Sue Gladstone
Production Hazel Kirkman

Editorial Director Kate Cave
Art Director Caroline Hillier
Head of Pictures Anne Fraser

Photographic Acknowledgments

a=above b=below l=left c=centre d=designer

The Garden Picture Library/Ron Sutherland 23

Rachel White 30-31

Jerry Harpur 18-19 (d: Stephen Suzman, San Francisco); 19r (d: Edwina von Gal, New York); 35b (d: Keith Corlett, New York); 45a (d: Victor Nelson, New York); 55 (d: Jim Matsuo, Los Angeles); 74a (d: Victor Nelson, New York); 79cr (d: R. David Adams, Seattle)

Andrew Lawson/designer Anthony Noel 1; 2-3; 4l; 5c; 10-11; 14-15; 16-17; 20-21; 24-25; 26-27; 28; 29l; 38-39; 42-43; 46-47; 48l; 49; 54a; 62-63; 64-65; 68-69; 70-71; 72-73; 73r; 74b; 75; 78-79; 80l; 82al; 82bl; 84; 85; 86-87; 88al; 88-89; 90-91; 97; 102-103; 114-115; 116-117; 119; 120-121; 122-123; 124-125

Andrew Lawson 4cl (d: James Aldridge); 5r; 7; 10l (Hidcote Manor, Gloucestershire); 16l (Haseley Court, Oxfordshire); 22l, 22r (Hidcote Manor, Gloucestershire); 32l (Blenheim Palace, Oxfordshire); 32r (Chatsworth, Derbyshire); 33 (The Priory, Charlbury, Oxfordshire); 35a (d: Paul Bangay, Melbourne); 35a, 39r & 40-41 (d: Paul Bangay, Melbourne); 50-51; 52 (Dalemain, Cumbria); 54c; 54b; 56-57; 58l; 58-59 (Lime Kiln Rosarium); 60; 61a; 61b (Whichford Pottery, Warwickshire); 66-67 (The Priory, Charlbury, Oxfordshire); 71r (d: Paul Bangay, Melbourne); 76 (d: George Carter); 77; 83br (Bourton House, Gloucestershire); 94; 95; 96; 98-99; 99ar; 99br; 100-101; 103ar; 103br; 105al; 105ar; 106-107; 108-109; 110-111; 113

Tony Lord 9

Clive Nichols 4cr (d: Anthony Noel); 5l (d: Anthony Noel); 41r & 42l (d: Natural & Oriental Water Gardens, Lighting by Garden & Security Lighting); 45b (d: Lisette Pleasance); 53 (ceramics by Dennis Fairweather); 68l (d: Sue Berger); 72a (d: Anthony Noel); 79ar (d: Lisette Pleasance); 79br (d: Anthony Noel); 81l (d: Anthony Noel); 83ar (d: Stephen Woodhams); 92-93 (d: Anthony Noel); 118 (Château de Villandry, France)

Steve Wooster 4-5 (d: Anthony Noel); 12-13 (d: Anthony Noel); 34-35 (d: Arabella Lennox-Boyd); 36 (d: Anthony Noel); 37a (Te Mara); 37b; 44 (d: Anthony Paul); 80r (d: Anthony Noel); 81r (d: Anthony Noel); 82-83 (d: Anthony Noel); 104-105 (d: Dan Pearson)